February 26, 2000

For Edward and Dzoing,

I want to thank Edward especially for creating such a beautiful memory for my sister to wear, and I thank you, Dzoing, for obviously making Edward so happy — which memory h̶ a smile on.

ID0950029

May your memories grow together,

Hermine Hilton

*The Surefire Way to Remember
Names, Numbers, and
Important Information*

THE
EXECUTIVE
MEMORY
GUIDE

Hermine Hilton

SIMON AND SCHUSTER   NEW YORK

Copyright © 1986 by Hermine Hilton
All rights reserved
including the right of reproduction
in whole or in part in any form
Published by Simon and Schuster
A Division of Simon & Schuster, Inc.
Simon & Schuster Building
Rockefeller Center
1230 Avenue of the Americas
New York, New York 10020
SIMON AND SCHUSTER and colophon are registered trademarks of
Simon & Schuster, Inc.

Designed by Eve Kirch
Manufactured in the United States of America

1   3   5   7   9   10   8   6   4   2

Library of Congress Cataloging-in-Publication Data
Hilton, Hermine, date
The executive memory guide.
1. Memory. 2. Mnemonics. 3. Businessmen—
Psychology. I. Title.
BF371.H55   1986   153.1'4   86-17878
ISBN: 0-671-60739-1

*This book is dedicated with love
to my mother, Augusta,
whom everyone would like to memorize.*

CONTENTS

INTRODUCTION

The Seven-Second Syndrome

Have you ever been introduced to someone at a business meeting and by the time you said "Hello" and were introduced to the next person you had already forgotten the first person's name?

Have you ever dialed a telephone number and then forgotten whom it was you were calling?

Have you ever had an important thought flash through your mind during a conversation and, not wanting to interrupt, waited till it was appropriate for you to speak, only to forget what you wanted to say?

Have you ever called your broker for a quote and, by the time you hung up, forgot the price he gave you?

Well, if you have experienced any or all of these embarrassing lapses, don't worry. There's nothing seriously wrong with your memory, and your problem is not unique. In fact, it's not even a problem. These lapses are merely cases of the Seven-Second Syndrome. When a person fails to "lock in" new information, it can be lost in as little as seven seconds. Lock it or lose it.

Fortunately, learning how to lock in new data is easy. And the chapters that follow will show you how.

In today's fast-paced business world, executives need fast-paced memories. The executive's mind and memory are at the heart of high-powered business meetings, delicate negotiating sessions, and even casual luncheons with colleagues. The busy executive needs to process information as rapidly as a computer. As you know from your own experience, the key to success is the quick, accurate storage and retrieval of facts, figures, names, and faces. There isn't always time to wait till you get back to the office to look something up or put in a call to your secretary to check the latest statistics. You need facts, and you need them fast.

Absentmindedness can hurt business more than absenteeism. When an employee is sick or on vacation, someone else can fill in. But when your memory is out to lunch, there is no temporary help. In most cases, only you know what you know, and it's up to you to deliver. Whether you want to remember the stock-market quotes you heard on the radio driving to work, the key points of a presentation you hope to give with an air of competence and authority, or the twenty-five-plus names and faces of the people you just met at a convention, you're often on your own to mentally file the facts where they can be easily accessed.

There's no such thing as a bad memory, only untrained ones. Many of us treat our memories like inexperienced junior executives—eager to learn but unreliable. An untrained memory can become a costly liability. Fortunately, it doesn't take years of experience to train your memory to be a powerful business asset. If you have trouble locking in new information, it's possible that you haven't found the right key, or perhaps the lock is just a bit rusty from years of disuse. All that's needed is a little polish, a few new keys—and you can stop blaming forgetfulness on a rusty memory.

MNEMONICS

With today's computers and high-speed communication technologies, it's surprising that more people are not familiar with the term *mnemonics*. (Perhaps it's one of those words you remember having heard somewhere, but whose meaning you just can't recall. If we give you a moment, you'll think of it, right?)

Mnemonic (pronounced ne-MON-ic; the first *m* is silent) comes from the Greek word meaning "of the mind." The Greek goddess Mnemosyne ruled the memory in the ancient Hellenic world, and today she reigns over the intricate workings of the computer. All computer programs use mnemonic codes to store and retrieve information much like the human mind, which invented the computer in the first place.

Mnemonics is the science of organizing new information and filing it in the mind by connecting it to known information for easy recall. The connection itself is the mnemonic.

Mnemonics is the exact opposite of learning by rote, mechanical repetition that involves little or no intelligence. While rote may be perfect for learning physical skills such as serving a tennis ball or swinging a golf club, it is of no use for learning intelligible data. You may recall "roting" during a cram session in college the night before a big exam, but the proof that rote memory involves very little *intelligent remembering* is clearly seen in how little of what you crammed is still with you and how insecure it made you feel. For short-term memory, rote may temporarily lock in a few facts, but they quickly slide into oblivion.

There is a big difference between repetition and genuine learning. Mere repetition produces no long-term memory. How often have you seen a Lincoln penny, and how much would you bet that you know which direction Old Abe faces?

THE MIND'S EAR

It's possible that after years of looking at pennies you are still uncertain which direction Lincoln faces, but if someone once *told* you that he faces right, the chances are you would still remember it. Why? Because for much information the mind's ear is a more important tool than the much-written-about mind's eye. In fact, most of what we need to remember is not visual at all. Stock prices, end-of-the-year statistics, the names of people—even when seen written on a page, the letters and numbers don't really stimulate the mind's eye.

Even though the initial impact of seeing is said to be fifty times stronger than that of any other sense, what is seen is often not slated for longevity. We see and forget. The message from the ear to the mind is more direct and longer lasting. In fact, an auditory message to the mind's ear can propagate a visual image en route.

For example, if you were told not to visualize a pink elephant, chances are before you could say "Okay, I won't" you'd have seen one. You may not want to admit that you see a pink elephant, but there it is. Similarly, the most futile words a judge can say in a jury trial are "Strike that from the record." By the time the words are uttered, twelve mental ears may have already recorded it, maybe with a visual image to boot!

Just as the principles of time management are crucial to the efficient working of an office, a department, or an entire company, managing internal time—mental time—is equally important. It is a waste of time to have to read the same memo more than once or look up information again and again simply because you haven't filed it mentally. By developing a "phonographic" memory, you can shorten the time you spend processing information because the mind's ear is the quickest and sharpest entry to the intellect. The mind's ear is thought itself.

DON'T JOKE ABOUT YOUR MEMORY

We talk about our memories in curious ways. An executive I met recently referred to his memory as "a nemesis on the premises." Often even relatively young executives after forgetting a name or fact, joke about "early senility" or "Alzheimer's disease." Most likely, you too have muttered the old adage, "In one ear and out the other," and then laughed as if it didn't matter. But it does. Joking about memory is no laughing matter. Not because there's nothing that can be done for your memory, but because the subconscious, where 90 percent of our memories are stored, doesn't have a sense of humor. It takes things literally. Wisecracks about a rusty memory or jokes about absentmindedness can be self-fulfilling. What I call "pseudosenility" can actually be brought on by a belief, even stated in jest, that it is inevitable. Memory does not have to fade with age.

There is no such thing as a "bad memory for this" or "a terrible memory for that." Don't even say it! Comments such as these send directives to the subconscious. As Shakespeare put it, "There is nothing either good or bad but thinking makes it so." Those "put downs" about your memory can harm you.

MENTAL NETWORKING

Networking is a powerful business tool, but you won't get the most out of it if you take the attitude that you need to connect with only 10 percent of the people you meet or capitalize on only 10 percent of the opportunities that come your way. Well, mental networking follows the same rules. You can't use only 10 percent of your brain, or just the right or the left brain, even though you consider yourself to lean in one or the other direction. Like joking about memory, thinking about yourself as left-brained or right-brained programs the unconscious to function in that very manner.

Using only part of the brain—letting a portion of the mind stagnate—is not conducive to learning, and learning is the key to survival in the corporate world. A newly hired junior executive may think there is a lot to learn, but the seasoned executive will readily admit that learning never stops. Mnemonic techniques can build the connections between bits of information that make learning easier. Unless what you learn is consciously stored in your memory, available for instant recall, you haven't really learned it. Mnemonic strategies can trigger the chain reaction that is often expressed as "and that reminds me." If your own retrieval systems seem rusty, applying mnemonic principles can create alternative paths for pulling out the information you need when you need it.

MEMORY ISN'T MAGIC

People often ask me to teach them some memory tricks as if calling forth remembered facts is like pulling rabbits out of empty hats. But memory recall utilizes conscious mental strategy, not intellectual sleight of hand, the supernatural, or what the old vaudeville posters called "extraordinary powers of concentration."

Recalling quantities of information may look like a mental feat, but it involves no trickery. For the truth of the matter is that the mind is definitely quicker than the eye, and without resorting to the mysterious, you can improve your memory abilities with reliable commonsense techniques based on the latest research in mnemonics. Recent studies emphasize the power and value of mnemonics. Experiments with university students using mnemonics produced memory retention and retrieval results hundreds of percentage points higher than those using rote or linking bizarre visual associations.

A curious phenomenon in Japan is the use of special "cram schools" called *juku* where extra training is given to help students pass their examinations. The *juku* method is based entirely on memory drills or rote and has nothing to do with understanding a subject. Thirty percent of all students from elementary school through junior high attend *juku* classes after school. But like American methods of cramming, *juku* results in very little retention once the examination is over. A rather unfortunate side effect of the rigorous testing in the Japanese educational system is the large number of students who commit suicide either before exams or after failing them. No wonder they refer to this period in life as "examination hell." Perhaps for these students mnemonics *would* be akin to magic.

CONCLUSION

This book is written to train you, the executive, in the latest mnemonic strategies for better memory. It includes both basic and advanced techniques that can be applied to any business situation where you need to be on top to stay at the top. Whether remembering names at a meeting, locking in seminar ideas, recalling facts from the *Wall Street Journal*, giving dynamic speeches and presentations without notes, or ordering lunches from a French menu, the executive who has mastered details inspires confidence that he or she can also master the larger picture.

In the pages that follow you'll discover ways to create mental connections between new ideas and what you already know by means of simple mnemonic techniques such as acronyms, acrostics, and the Mnumeric Alphabet. Once you've mastered these basics, you can incorporate their principles into a more comprehensive mnemonic strategy called the Master Code that will assist you in remembering truly astounding quantities of information, including statistical data, with amazing speed. There is no occult knowledge or esoteric principle for developing a sharp memory. Nor is there some rare talent inherited by only a few individuals. On the contrary, a great memory is based on very practical, commonsense procedures that can be learned by anyone.

1

Locking In Ideas

*Lock in the thought of the moment during
the moment of the thought.*

SCENARIO

The alarm goes off, and in the five-minute snooze period
you get a flash of inspiration. Joe Bart in public relations!
Why hadn't you thought of him while you lay awake half
the night stewing about the problem that's been plaguing
you for weeks? Bart is the ideal person to handle it. You
make a mental note to call him as soon as you get to the
office because he'll be leaving at 11:00 A.M. for a national
public-relations conference on the Coast. Then five minutes
are up, the alarm goes off again. You hop out of bed and
into the shower, feeling better than you have in weeks. At
breakfast your children barrage you with questions and
"May-I's," and they're amazed that you're in such a good
mood. In fact, you feel great. Joe Bart is the answer to your
problem. You leave a little early and drive the shortcut so
you can prepare yourself before soliciting Joe's assistance.

19

But when you arrive, your secretary has a list of calls you should return. She also reminds you of some important matters that stacked up yesterday afternoon and that require immediate attention. Before you know it, the clock reads 11:05 and you realize Joe Bart is on his way to the airport.

Where did you go wrong? How could you have forgotten, when Bart's assistance was so important to you?

THE PROBLEM

The problem is a common one: losing a valuable idea. It's normal for most of us to lose ideas in the course of a busy day, even about important matters. When you have that gnawing thought "There's something important I'm supposed to do," you're probably right. There is! Now if you could just make that idea—which you know is tucked away somewhere in your memory—come to the surface.

I know one executive who carries a three-by-five notebook, which he calls his "idea trap." He uses it to capture ideas whenever they occur. He's even been known to swerve across six lanes on the Los Angeles freeway to pull over onto the shoulder and jot down an idea. He's convinced that what he calls his "fifty-ounce biocomputer of a brain" just won't come through in a pinch. Well, you don't have to risk your life in heavy traffic just to hang on to an idea.

Losing ideas, even in traffic, is not a memory problem but a retrieval problem. Most thoughts are extremely fleeting and will sink into unconscious oblivion unless you know the secret of locking them in for retrieval. Unfortunately, none of us were born with the skill. Most of what happens to us never comes back to consciousness, and that may be a blessing! With extreme methods of recall, such as hypnosis, a lot of that old material can be stirred up, even in the smallest detail. But even with a secretary who knows hypnosis, you probably don't want to "go under" each morning just to remember the brilliant ideas that occurred to you overnight!

Such drastic methods are not necessary. Everyone can learn simple mnemonic strategies for locking in new ideas when they occur so that they are readily available for recall when needed. The mind is a vast network of information, and anyone can develop the skill to organize that information with connectors that will activate and extract the necessary data.

The memory collects information in two distinct ways: consciously and unconsciously. The basic difference is that, in the conscious process, we control the storing of information. When we abdicate this control, the unconscious will most likely swallow up the information, making it much more difficult to retrieve. The unconscious mind collects anything and everything, naturally and without our assistance. It retains its power over these bits and pieces of knowledge and will not easily release them. Often strenuous mental effort on our part won't help. I'm sure you know how quickly you can worry a fact or a name out of reach. The more you grab for it mentally, the more it seems to slide away. You're like the quiz-show contestant who knows the answer but can't bring it to mind.

The unconscious is not a good team player.

Conscious memory, however, is an ally. It puts us in control, making it easier for us to activate memories and retrieve them from the unconscious. When we consciously collect new knowledge, we connect it to what we already know. It's a simple process of collecting and connecting, and the result is that we are in control of re-collecting. The old phrase "It's right on the tip of my tongue" is a slightly misapplied metaphor. It should be "It's right on the tip of my mind." You actually mean that what you are trying to remember is on the tip of the unconscious but just below conscious awareness. If only you could boot it up another level, you would have it.

THE SOLUTION

How can we take conscious control of recall? By learning to make conscious mnemonic connections *before* we store anything away. In other words, by connecting unfamiliar information to familiar. We program prompter cues. We create strong mental connections between the new and known.

A mnemonic connection works somewhat like a physical association. The old folk method of tying a string around a finger to remember something is a physical application of the same idea. However, the weakness of this method is clearly seen in the joke about the absentminded person who couldn't remember *why* the string was there! There is no logical connection between string and most of the things we need to remember. Perhaps the need to buy a new roll of string is the exception!

A more logical association would be turning an ashtray upside down on your desk to remind you to empty the garbage or setting your empty vitamin bottle on the dresser to remind yourself to buy a new supply.

Mnemonic connections work on the same principle. They

are clear, logical mental associations to remind us of what we need to know.

In our opening scenario about forgetting an important detail such as Joe Bart's leaving town at 11:00 A.M., you might have locked in that crucial fact with the phrase "seven-eleven." As you hurried off to work in the morning thinking how lucky you were to have come up with a solution to your problem, you could have made the mental connection between "lucky" and the gambler's call "seven-eleven" to remind you that your success depended on "calling" Bart by 11:00 A.M. But you did nothing to lock in that fact, and in the course of the morning other important matters drove it into your unconscious, where it became inoperative. You may not have *remembered* this fact in time to use it, but you can't truly say that you actually *forgot* it. You just couldn't retrieve it. It never connected to a place in your memory where it was available for recall.

Let's say that while you are at dinner in a restaurant you get an idea for the title of a speech you have to give, but you don't want to take time out from your dinner conversation to write it down. If the title is "Fine-Tuning Your Job," you could create a mental picture of a piano tuner doing his *job* tuning your piano.

Or suppose that, while driving, you come up with an idea for a company logo using the infinity symbol. Just imagine your car ice-skating around freeways performing figure eights. That will remind you of the infinity symbol.

One last example. You hear an interesting ad on the radio that might prove to be a good commercial venture for your company, and you want to remember the station you heard it on. If it is station CFOX, turn the letters into a sentence: "See (C) the *fox* wearing earphones." Or see (C) the radio announcer as a "*foxy* lady," or picture yourself buying a Canadian red-*fox* coat for your foxy wife.

CONCLUSION

Locking in ideas is a three-step process:

First, be aware of the necessity to lock in new ideas. Don't just have ideas. Do something *consciously* with them so you retain control over their retrieval.

Second, make a mental connection by thinking of a strong idea or image that has a logical association with the new idea.

Third, rethink the connection for recall.

2

Absent Mind-edness

Your age has nothing to do with the fact that you can't find your keys.

SCENARIO

It hasn't been the best of all possible days. You're sure you got out of bed on one side and your brain got out on the other. Not only did you waste twenty minutes looking for your keys before leaving for work—only to find them on the television, right where you put them late last night—but now you can't find your car in the multistoried parking garage downtown. Your first thought is that it might be stolen. You know you should have taken time to check which level and what aisle you parked in before heading for your attorney's office, but you were late for the appointment and his hourly rates seem to go up every other week so you didn't want to take the time. Now there's nothing to do but start on the second level. (You're certain you didn't park on the ground level because that would mean something was going *right* today and anyway you remember

getting dizzy from circling around so many times before
you found a place. Even if you could remember how many
times you circled around, it still wouldn't indicate the level
because parking-garage architecture is perverse.) You remember an old joke about lost items always turning up in
the last place you look. Why? Because then you stop looking! But you don't think it's very funny. Not today. Today
nothing is funny.

THE PROBLEM

The problem is absentmindedness, which afflicts all of us at
one time or another, some of us more than others, on some
days more than others. I have met people who are convinced
it has something to do with atmospheric pollution, full
moons, or earthquakes in remote parts of the earth. The
truth is that it's no one's fault but our own. *We* do the
things that get us into those scrapes where we feel foolish
because we have forgotten something so obvious or important that we never took the time to remember it. Let that
be the first principle: The importance or obviousness of any
given fact is no guarantee that you will remember it.

   Absentmindedness is a literal term. It is actually a condition
characterized by the mind's being absent from an action.
Put another way, it is the thought's being absent from the
mind. However you view it, all three must be actively
present in order to remember the details of daily life: a
mind, thinking clearly and dynamically, about an *action*.
Only in certain Zen practices is "no-mind" an asset. For
most of us in our daily routines, no-mind leads to confusion
and embarrassment, not enlightenment.

Furthermore, absentmindedness has nothing to do with intelligence or age. The presidents of colleges can be as absentminded as the proverbial professors, and eighteen-year-old freshmen sometimes honestly leave their term papers on their desks in the dorm. It can happen to anyone, and studies show that it does. Everyone suffers moments of forgetfulness.

At the core of the problem is a simple fact: the mind needs assistance. Attention must be focused. Given the multitude of tasks we must perform every day, our minds would go berserk if we had to attend consciously to each one. A switching-off mechanism in the brain allows us to handle many daily tasks without thinking about them. We say they are habitual. Some of us view them as rituals; others see them as ruts. A problem arises when we need to be consciously aware of them but, because our minds take the easy way out, we switch them off.

The mind can be like a photographer snapping pictures left and right at an important function, only to discover later that there was no film in the camera. Our eyes often operate in a similar fashion, and we shouldn't be misled into thinking that because we looked at something we really saw it or that because we saw it we will automatically remember it. The eye can only see, it can't remember; and much of what passes through the eyes in the course of a day is only looked at. It isn't really "seen."

When you suffer from absentmindedness, don't let it get you down. If you let it become a source of worry or stress, you will only compound the problem. What your mind needs is relaxation and conscious focusing, not unnecessary stewing and fretting. Additional worries will only unfocus the mind even more, causing you to forget or overlook even more things.

THE SOLUTION

You've heard the advice "Put your money where your mouth is." To overcome forgetfulness, put your mind where your action is. Sometimes this can be difficult because we have so many habitual activities that we perform without thinking about them. But force yourself to attend to the ones where it is important for you to remember something, like where you place your keys or where you park your car. Put your mind into those actions and force yourself to create a mental connection that will bring the details of that act back into focus. Eventually, making these mental connections will become as habitual as the activities themselves. Like any new skill, it just takes time and practice.

There are two types of mental connections for overcoming absentmindedness. But before we learn them, let's consider a few facts about the process of making mental connections. Psychologically, *any* connection will work because the act of making a connection in itself slows you down and focuses your attention on what you are doing. It brings your conscious attention to what you want to remember. In some memory theories you are told to create bizarre images and associations because they will bring the memory back more vividly. I'm convinced that's not necessarily true. In my experience, people remember better with logical, clever connections that are direct and to the point. They needn't be outlandish associations that have only a ridiculous relationship to the situation. Nevertheless, any connection that activates your imagination and brings your awareness to what you are doing, to what you want to remember, is valid. The reason a consciously wrought connection will help you remember is that in the process of creating the connection you are creating the memory itself. Consciously "making" the important events of the day will help you remember them better than if you just let them "happen" to you.

Two types of mental connections are handy for remembering the daily details that are so easy to forget. The first is visualization; the second is what I call "mental memos."

You may have noticed that absentmindedness frequently occurs in situations that have strong visual components. Unlike remembering facts, figures, and dates, the daily activities that slip our minds are usually little dramatic scenarios in themselves. Dropping keys on a table, leaving a letter to be mailed on your desk, forgetting where you stuck your umbrella when you went into someone's office— these and similar actions can breed forgetfulness because we fail to activate the visual component that is really there. We literally need to focus our attention upon it, see it mentally, photograph it in our minds. Visualization is a powerful tool for connecting routine events to the memory.

You may need to learn visualization step by step if you have never used it before. First, clear your mind of other images. Then visualize what you need to remember—the keys on the television, the umbrella behind the door. It often helps to add one other detail to enrich the visualization. For example, if you see a magazine rack behind the door, add that to your image. Or notice the cover of the *TV Guide* right next to the keys. Often this related detail will really lock the image into your memory. Then as you turn your back or walk away, continue mentally to *see* the image for a moment until the mind moves on to its next task. Of course, as you use visualization to remember what you are doing, you won't have to take it step by step. It will happen instantaneously, like a camera snapping a picture.

Try this the next time you lay something down, whether keys, glasses, wallet, or whatever. Flash the mind a picture, turn away, and still *see* the item when your back is turned.

Conversely, if you've ever "forgotten what I came here for," use visualization for situations that involve your going for something, such as down to the lounge for a cup of coffee or to the corporate library for a special issue of a journal. When you first get the idea, picture yourself at the spot performing the task. See yourself with the cup of coffee or reaching up to the shelf for the journal. In your mind's eye, visualize yourself having already achieved what you are going for. Then repeat the image immediately before you set off, as you get up from your desk or leave your office.

A second tool for overcoming absentmindedness is writing a mental memo. For short-term memory such as remembering where you parked your car, mentally "write" yourself a reminder in some imaginative way. You might use a rhyme, jingle, pun, or any clever play on words.

For example, if you parked near a tavern, create a jingle such as "I parked my car near Clancy's Bar."

Check the cross streets and devise a mental connection between them. If it was near the corner of Maple Street and Second Avenue, you might write: "I'm parked between two maples."

Can you find a pun in the name of the street? If you parked on Wilshire Boulevard, you can turn it into "Welsh ire" and imagine a furious Welshman haranguing you for taking his parking space.

Notice the aisle number and color code in parking garages and create some imaginative connection between the two. For example, level blue, aisle B could be turned into "don't Be BLUE." Level green, aisle D might suggest "a GREENback Dollar."

EXERCISES

The only way to learn mnemonic strategies like these is to do them, but before you implement them in your actual activities, it would be wise to practice on some right now. Take a few minutes and decide how you could visualize or write mental memos for the following situations:

- placing your keys in the usual spot in your home
- remembering that, after reading a file, you put it down on a cluttered desk
- remembering that, after saying good-bye to a new client who gives you his card, you immediately stick it in your jacket pocket
- wondering where you will stash your umbrella at tomorrow's business meeting
- remembering to stop by the lounge to get a cup of coffee on your way back from the legal department
- remembering to run down to the company library for a copy of last year's annual report
- remembering to buy theater tickets before you come back from lunch

Here is how I would remember the first three situations and the last:

If I put the keys in the ashtray on the dining-room table, I would visualize the keys in the ashtray instead of cigarette butts. A mnemonic connection between the two might be the thought that this is a "key reminder" to give up smoking.

After laying the file on a cluttered desk, I would visualize it drowning in the "out" box.

As I put the client's card in my pocket, I would think of my pocket as a card file with this rhyme on it: "Always lock it in your pocket."

To remember to buy theater tickets before coming back from lunch, I would visualize paying two bills at lunch, one for lunch and one for the theater. Later, when I actually paid the lunch bill, that would be a reminder that I must also stop to buy theater tickets.

CONCLUSION

The solution to remembering where you put things or what you have to do is really very simple. Create a mental picture or a mental memo and relax. Even on the busiest days you can retain an air of calm and control, reduce absentmindedness and the stress and embarrassment that come with it. With practice, creating mental connections for even the most routine activities will become so commonplace that you'll never fail to lock them in.

3

Remembering TTDT
(Things To Do Today)

Don't come undone when something's undone.

SCENARIO

You're running late today because the traffic is snarled on
the interstate. Finally you see your exit and you know that,
barring bottlenecks in the downtown area, you should be in
your office in fifteen minutes. Then it occurs to you. You
can't remember locking the front door! You mentally try to
re-see yourself dashing out of the house, hoping to trigger
a visual memory of locking the door behind you, but nothing comes. Blank! Then, because doubts seem to multiply
like cars in downtown traffic, you wonder if you put your
weekly organizer in your briefcase. You could lean over the
seat and pop your briefcase open, but the last time you did
that in heavy traffic—*this* you can remember!—you almost
had an accident. So you decide to wait till you get to your
parking lot. In the last half block, your composure (what's
left of it) slips even further as you remember that you defi-

nitely did not turn on the telephone-answering machine in your study. And as you pull into the parking lot, you can't resist touching your coat pocket where you keep your wallet to feel that reassuring bulge. It's there, and you compliment yourself on not having left your wallet at home two days in a row!

THE PROBLEM

It's not the daily basics that are the problem. It's remembering both *to do* them and *if you did* them. Worrying because you can't remember if you did them can be almost as aggravating as recalling that you forgot to do them. Actually, this is another form of absentmindedness that occurs to everyone at some time or other, and almost always on the way to the airport.

Many executives claim there are two times they usually find themselves thinking about the things they have to include in their business day: at night before falling asleep and in the morning while shaving or putting on makeup. They feel secure in the fact that they remember and can plan ahead, but sadly, many admit that no matter how well they make their mental lists and go over them in their heads, they still forget an item or two. Remembering "things to do today"—whether business or personal tasks —needs some kind of pre-applied mental organization with some *MNEMONIC* clout!

Ideally, you should have a permanent checklist that includes the tasks you need to do each day, such as locking the door, taking your wallet, packing your briefcase. In addition, you need a system for creating checklists on an ad hoc basis wherever and whenever tasks occur to you. To be able to do this mentally is an asset because you can't always reach for paper and pen while you're driving down the highway or running to catch a plane, which seems to be the ultimate activity for creating stress and worry over forgetting important matters.

THE SOLUTION

Fortunately, a simple yet effective method for remembering lists of TTDT (Things To Do Today) is the use of *acronyms* and *acrostics*.

An *acronym* is a word formed from the first letters of the words that make up a phrase. Not every acronym reproduces the meaning of the phrase it stands for, but some do so very cleverly. GASP stands for Group Against Smog and Pollution. MADD is Mothers Against Drunk Drivers, and MOUSE stands for Minimal Orbital Unmanned Satellite of Earth. EGADS is Electronic Ground Automatic Destruct System, a signal given to intercept an in-flight missile. VIOLENT is Viewers Intent On Listing Episodes on Nationwide Television.

Other acronyms may not be actual words or have an obvious meaning that relates to what they stand for. Nevertheless, with time, the good ones can become as well known as the others. WACs were members of the Women's Army Corps during World War II. ASAP means As Soon As Possible. SAC stands for the Strategic Air Command. ZIP, as in zip code, originally meant Zone Improvement Program. You are probably already familiar with the contemporary business acronyms, OPM (Other People's Money),

SOP (Standard Operating Procedures), PMA (Positive Mental Attitude), and KISS (Keep It Simple, Stupid!).

An acronym is a kind of abbreviation, a device for using a part for the whole, and since the individual letters hang together as a bona fide word (SANE: Safe Alternatives to Nuclear Energy) or as a sound that comes close to being a word (EPCOT: Experimental Prototype Community Of Tomorrow), it's easy to remember. What's more, by recalling the single word, you recall all the parts.

If you were the executive driving to work in our opening scenario, you could have gotten a load off your mind by using the acronym LOAD:

L —Lock door
O—Organizer
A—Answering machine
D—Dollar

This simple mnemonic could be used every morning to assure remembering these four tasks.

Here's an acronym for the contents of a woman's tote bag: MAKEUP. If we break the acronym down by letter, each of which stands for an item in the bag, we have:

M—Makeup
A —Address book
K—Keys
E —Executive wallet
U—Umbrella
P —Perfume

Make a list of the routine things you have to do each morning before you leave for work or after you get to work and devise an acronym for them.

Keep in mind that if the tasks can be done in any order, you can rearrange the first letter of each task until you find a suitable word. If possible, make a real word, like LOAD, or a combination of letters that can be pronounced as a "pseudoword." For example, if you were making an ad hoc acronym for things to do on your way home today—

pick up the laundry
buy theater tickets for the weekend
stop by the gym

—you would have the letters L, T, and G for laundry, tickets, and gym. Arranged as GLT, these suggest the sound *glit,* which should be easy to remember.

If the letters can't be arranged to suggest a word or even a pronounceable sound, try using alternative terms for one or two items. For example, *gym* could be *exercise,* the E helping to make LET (laundry, exercise, tickets).

Sometimes neither a word nor a pronounceable sound can be made, but the letters have some consistency or relationship in themselves. These same three tasks could become CCC if the play you were going to buy tickets for was *A Chorus Line,* and you used *club* for *health club* and *clothes* for laundry. As you can see, several variations are possible for any list of tasks.

You shouldn't have trouble devising an acronym for the things you have to do every day. The tasks that change from day to day, however, may not fit easily into an acronym, or you may not have time to devise one. Also, it may be difficult to invent an acronym for a large number of tasks, say eight, nine, ten, or more. Suitable nine- and ten-letter words may not spring immediately to mind. In this case, an acrostic is often a better choice for a mnemonic.

An *acrostic* is an initialing strategy similar to the acronym, but the letters form words in a sentence. Although this may sound more complicated than forming a single word, it really isn't. Not every word need stand for a task the way each letter in the acronym must. And you have more room for invention since each letter can stand for an almost infinite number of words. You're limited only by the extent of your own vocabulary.

Here are two examples. "My Very Economical Mother Just Saved Us Nine Percent" is an acrostic for remembering the names of the planets in our solar system and their order from the sun: Mercury, Venus, Earth, Mars, Jupiter, Saturn, Uranus, Neptune, and Pluto. Psychology students have remembered the four varieties of schizophrenia with the acrostic "Sick Campers Pack Heavily": simple, catatonic, paranoid, and hebephrenic. This acrostic has an additional built-in mnemonic in that you can remember the sentence by thinking of schizophrenics as having a heavy load to carry.

If you had the following list of TTDT—

1. Get suit pressed
2. Check private postal box
3. Transfer funds to a money-market account
4. Sign corporate papers by five o'clock
5. Check agency ad in *Business Week*
6. Sign finance report
7. Send estimated tax forms to accountant

—you could create a sentence like
     "Sometimes Playing Monopoly Can Be Fun Too"

or
     "Some People May Cancel Before Friday's Test."

Both sentences (and there are others that would work just as well) come from the first letter of the important word in each task:

Suit—S
P.O. box—P
Money market—M
Corporate papers—C
Business Week—B
Finance report—F
Tax forms—T

If you must do these tasks in the order given, leave them as they are. However, if the order doesn't matter, you can rearrange them to make an easier sentence.

As an exercise, take those seven letters and create your own sentence.

Then take the following tasks and write an acrostic or two for them:

Call Marvin
Buy cat food
Return books to library
Make airline reservations
Pick up computer disks
Order stationery
Call husband/wife
Buy birthday present for nephew

Suppose you are restocking your office library and want to include new business books on these topics: Consulting, Contracts, Letter writing, Management, Marketing, Memory, Strategy, Time Management. Study the following acrostics to learn how these topics can be used to form several sentences.

"3 Maidens Lead 2 Cows To Salinas."

M—Memory
M—Management
M—Marketing
L —Letter writing
C —Consulting
C —Contracts
T —Time management
S —Strategy

(The three maidens and the two cows remind us there are three M topics and two C topics.)

"3 Managers Laughingly Signed Terrific Consulting Contracts."

M—Management
M—Marketing
M—Memory
L —Letter writing
S —Strategy
T —Time management
C —Consulting
C —Contracts

(Use the three managers to give you the three M topics, and use two actual topics, Consulting and Contracts, as words in the acrostic.)

"My My My This Cold City Loves Snow."

M—Marketing
M—Memory
M—Management
T —Time management

C —Contracts
C —Consulting
L —Letter writing
S —Strategy

(In this acrostic, the initial letter of each word represents a topic.)

"My My My This Crafty Client Loves Strategy."

M—Marketing
M—Memory
M—Management
T —Time management
C —Contracts
C —Consulting
L —Letter writing
S —Strategy

(In this acrostic, also, the initial letter of each word represents a topic.)

Here are two acrostics to remind you to return calls today to Hunter, Ike, Elandra, Sheldon, and Unger:

"How Is Everything Shaping Up?"

H—Hunter
I —Ike
E —Elandra
S —Sheldon
U —Unger

You may want to reflect the order of importance of these calls in the acrostic:

"Everything Is Hot Until Sunday."

E —Elandra
I —Ike
H—Hunter
U—Unger
S —Sheldon

Sometimes, when remembering three or four items, you might find it easier—and more fun—simply to compose a sentence using each of the items rather than only their initial letters. For example, recently I had to go to the bank and the post office, buy a frozen fish dinner, and stop by my health club to jog. The order wasn't important. Almost immediately (because I invent these mnemonics out of habit, and you will too with a little practice) the following sentence occurred to me: "The *fish jogged* to the *post* on the *bank*."

CONCLUSION

Acronyms and acrostics are two of the simplest mnemonic devices for remembering lists of things to do. The underlying principle is the same; namely, convert the list to single words or their initials and recombine them in such a way that they are easy to remember. This might be a word, a pseudoword, or a sentence. If it takes you awhile initially to devise acronyms and acrostics, stick with it. It gets easier with practice. I've worked with executives who were convinced their imaginations weren't sharp enough to devise them. They were under the impression that their minds "just didn't work that way" and that coming up with clever words and sentences was not their talent. But in a very short time, by forcing themselves to put their daily tasks into acronyms and acrostics, they eventually found themselves *thinking* in initials and pieces of sentences! The same can happen to you.

4

"I Remember Your Face, But—"

What's in a name? Everything!

SCENARIO

You're at the first cocktail party of this year's convention and you've just disentangled yourself from a conversation that was beginning to wear rather thin. Complimenting yourself on having "moved on" without looking as if you were bored, you sidle over to a buffet for a canapé. As you reach for it, a vaguely familiar voice, booming with joviality, exclaims "Well, well, I can't believe it's you!" You look up at a bright, beaming face that you remember from —where? It smiles at you; a hand stretches out for a hearty shake. The congenial newcomer asks how you've been, using both your first and last names. You drop the canapé back on the tray, shift your drink to your left hand, shake hands with the not-quite stranger, not-quite acquaintance, and mutter something like "Well, well, is it really you?"

Surprisingly, you manage to exchange a string of "How

44

are you doing?" and "How is so-and-so?" comments until something he says reminds you that he was an important client several years ago with Fleming Industries. Now if you could just remember his name! You drop a "Fleming Industries" remark and he takes the bait. While he recites a litany of all the company's achievements over the past five years, you wrack your brain for his name. You try unsuccessfully to visualize the Fleming Industries card in your Rolodex. Nothing! Just when you think you've listened politely long enough and could offer a "moving on" comment, you see the chief executive officer of your company angling his way through the crowd. You've been at cocktail parties with him before, and you know from past experience that he'll expect an introduction. You feel like the proverbial trapped rat!

THE PROBLEM

Ninety-nine out of a hundred executives I meet tell me they have had trouble at one time or another remembering people's names. The majority admit to its being *most* of the time. On the other hand, they find they can usually remember a face, and wonder why this is. The answer is simple. Seeing the person's face again is a visual reminder in itself of what one has previously seen. You are, however, on your own, without any verbal reminder, to come up with the name.

The reason we have such a hard time remembering names, especially in unexpected encounters, is that usually the name wasn't "collected and connected" (learned consciously) in the first place and we get flustered by running into the person suddenly and simply suffer a mental block. The unconscious provides us no path to retrieval. The person could be someone we've worked with for years but whose name we just can't think of. Contrarily, we can sometimes remember names of people we've met only once. The fact that a name is unusual cannot be blamed, as uncommon or difficult names create more initial awareness, and thereby are often more readily recalled than the Smiths and Joneses, which are not attention-getting names. In fact, the old line "How do you pronounce (or spell) your name?" —which has gotten people out of scrapes like the scenario above—can backfire when the reply is a simple (and sarcastic) "J-O-N-E- S".

A rose by any other name would lose its identity no matter how convinced Juliet was to the contrary, and our personal identities are the most important things to most of us. After all, in a group photograph, whose face and name do you look for first? And how upset are you if the caption writer has transposed your name with that of the person standing at your side? Why do you enjoy taking clients to restaurants where the maitre d' calls you by name? The answer is obvious. Everyone's ego needs boosting, and the "sweetest sound" to anyone's ears is his or her name. The ability to remember names is power in itself. In business, and especially in sales, if we can remember the name, we have a head start in winning the other person over to our views.

Getting a name wrong, or forgetting it altogether, is an embarrassing lapse. When someone mispronounces your name or calls you by the wrong name, fancy verbal footwork is often necessary to correct the error without compounding the embarrassment. It's an awkward situation for both parties. In today's world, when so many of our business transactions are dependent upon whom we know and who knows us, it comes as a severe blow when someone you thought knew you well garbles your name. Being unable to come up with the right name can engender mistrust and loss of confidence. Don't compound the problem by saying, "I remember your face, I just can't remember your name." After all, in business we are out to make a name for ourselves, not a face.

Keeping this in mind, don't hesitate to ask someone to repeat his or her name after you've just been introduced to make sure you've heard it right. It is not necessarily a sign of the Seven-Second Syndrome. Rather, it can appear to be a compliment to the person that you really want to remember the name, lock it in, and not forget it. Besides, most people like to repeat their names.

THE SOLUTION: SOME "DON'TS"

Everyone has heard of some "foolproof" way to fix a name in your memory. Memory books are filled with bizarre and outrageous ways to make associations between names and faces, but I've discovered that many of the associations are misleading and create a false sense of security. A lot of them just don't work. They let you down when you really need them.

Here are a few "don'ts" that may keep you from being led the wrong way down memory lane:

NO WEIRD PICTURES

Don't try to create some bizarre visual image between the name and face of the person you are being introduced to. It

is what you are *hearing* that you should focus on. Spending
the first few seconds after an introduction trying to concoct
a weird mental connection between warts, pimples, glasses,
or widow's peaks and the name will usually only distract
your attention.

For example, if you meet a man named Trunk, don't try
to visualize an elephant on his head. Such a bizarre association isn't needed when you could come up with a more
logical picture, such as seeing him as an executive with so
much paper work that he carries it around in a trunk. Keep
your focus on the name you are hearing. Even ask him to
repeat it if necessary.

DON'T COUNT ON CLOTHES

Do not make a mental connection between the person's
name and what he or she is wearing. Most likely when you
meet the person again she won't be wearing the bright red
dress or he the exotic tie. Relying on clothes will only leave
you clueless the next time you meet.

DON'T WASTE TIME ON SHAPES, SIZES, AND FACIAL FEATURES

No matter how many different varieties of chins, noses,
ears, and mouths there are, energy spent trying to force a
connection between a pug nose or a pointed chin and a
name is usually wasted. Chances are the woman with the
widow's peak will not be named Mrs. Peak or Mrs. Widow.
In general, people's names and faces don't match.

DON'T DISTORT

You should look closely at the person's face but not to distort it with comic-strip features that are there only in your imagination. Name recall is activated by what is really there. You want to remember the face, warts and all, as it is. Relatable, relevant details will help you recognize it later, but by themselves they will not bring the name to mind. For the most part, the first feature that strikes you, or the first association that comes to mind, is the most reliable.

Of course, be attentive to the few times the face and the name do match. A Bitterman whose face is pinched like a pickle or a Fritz who looks as you've always pictured a Fritz have ready-to-go connections. But again, most people's faces do not match their names, just as most people's names do not match their occupations.

It's all right to imaginatively add some relevant contrasting feature to the face, if that will help you remember the name. For example, you might put a mole on the moleless face of Mr. Mole or add a ruddy complexion to the pale-skinned Miss Ruddy. It is always good to notice any outstanding features while you are connecting with the name because the visual and auditory senses can reinforce each other mentally. Just don't let your connections get out of hand.

DON'T REPEAT THE NAME OVER AND OVER

Repeating the name over and over, mechanically trying to pound it in, won't work. The eye and ear on their own do not do the learning. Remember, you wouldn't have staked your life on which way Lincoln faces on a penny! This is why so often you feel you've been paying close attention but suffer an attack of the Seven-Second Syndrome and forget the new name as soon as the next person is introduced to you.

You can solve the problem only by *doing* something conscious and meaningful with the name to lock it in for later recall.

THE SOLUTION: SOME "DO'S"

Now that you've seen the "don'ts," let's take a look at the "do's." Basically, there are four do's: (1) *categorize* names, (2) *substitute* related and meaningful words for them, (3) *link* first and last names to each other, and (4) *apply* results to the person in whatever way is appropriate whether it be looks, personality, behavior, or occupation.

CATEGORIZE

Categorizing is the surest way to learn and retain a new name because it makes an instant connection in the mind's ear. The auditory message travels the shortest route to the brain without wasting any time. If the sound of the name triggers a visual image along the way, consider that a bonus.

First, pay attention to both the person and the name. Look directly at the person, taking note of any outstanding features, and listen attentively to the name. Repeat the name aloud, making sure you have the correct pronunciation. If it is a long or foreign name, or one that is unfamiliar to you, you might ask the person to spell it. The extra time spent on the person's name will give you more time for creating the mnemonic connection that will lock it in your memory. If the spelling is not congruent with the pronunciation, ignore the spelling for the moment. You don't want to send mixed messages to the brain that might throw your pronunciation off. What's important at the moment is to pronounce it correctly in order to make an accurate connection. You aren't going to be writing a letter to the person yet. Correct spelling can come later.

Next, put the name mentally into one of the following categories:

1. *Do you know someone else with the same name?*
This is one of the easiest and best categories. There are two ways to go about this. First, if the name is the same as someone you know personally, use that as a category. It is a category of real-life experience, and putting the name into it places the new person in an old memory pattern. Second, the name may be similar to that of a celebrity or an historical or literary figure. Carson, Monroe, Beethoven, O'Hara, and similar names may readily call to mind famous persons, events, or historical periods that will help connect the new person to something with which you are already familiar.

2. *Does the name represent an occupation?*
Names such as Carpenter, Taylor, Presser, Singer, Hooker, Mason, and so forth can easily be fitted into an occupational category. Don't, however, expect the people you meet to do any of these things. Chances are they won't. Also, don't try to force a connection between their names and what you know their actual occupations to be. Most won't fit, and

the mental effort you expend on the exercise will distract
you from really locking in the name.

3. Does the name remind you of a color, object, or quality?
Names like Green, Brown, Ball, Hills, Kane, Church,
Sweet, and so forth can be remembered by connecting them
to familiar words in our daily conversation. You'll still have
to make a mental connection between the name and the
person. A Mr. Brown may not have brown hair. Miss
Church may look like she enjoys other activities on Sunday
mornings. In these cases, mentally note the contradiction.
If you need to do some mental "imagineering" by giving
Mr. Green green hair, do so. Just don't overdo it.

4. Is the name a famous brand name?
Campbell, Wilson, Johnson, Hilton will easily conjure up
the image of what they represent, and that should be an
effective connection. Keep in mind that you don't need to
create outlandish associations such as chicken-noodle soup
dripping down Mr. Campbell's chin or earlobes dangling
like tennis balls on Ms. Wilson's neck.

   You must, however, make a connection between what
your ear hears and what the mind hears if you want to
prevent the Seven-Second Syndrome. Without a mental association, the name will be gone before you know it.

5. Is the name that of a location?
A name the same or similar to a familiar place or geograph-
ical location has a built-in connection: London to London,
Downing to Downing Street, Caroline to the Carolinas.
Add a *ville, burg, port,* etc. to many names and you can
create your own connections, such as: Messrs. Steuben,

Vicks, and Williams could be hailing from Steubenville, Vicksburg, and Williamsport.

6. *Is the name a dictionary word of any kind?*
Any name that is also a standard dictionary word (or sounds like one) can be remembered easily by making the association between it and the noun, adjective, verb, or adverb that it reminds you of. Many people have names that are everyday words in themselves, such as North, Fale, Young, Pick, French, Grandleigh.

I've had people in my seminars with names like Fink, Floosie, Dickey, Doozy, Adhoc, and Glasscock. They weren't hard to make connections with and remember!

SUBSTITUTE

If the name won't fit into any workable category as it is, you may need to do some substituting. There are several ways to do this.

1. *Can you substitute a rhyming word for it?*
Connecting the name with an obvious rhyme often helps lock it in, especially if you can create a one- or two-line jingle using them. Then connect the thought in the rhyme in any way you can to the person, his or her looks, behavior, occupation, life-style, etc. For example, "Waldo Schlitches has the itches," "Jennifer Jix does her tricks," "Rachel Plenny hasn't any."

2. *Can you change the spelling slightly to make it mean something?*
For example, transpose Shaefer to shaver, Zebtic to septic, Kendle to candle, Bakall to bagel, Dressler to dresser, Kes-

sler to kisser. I once met a man named Kendle and mentally changed it to Candle because he owned a funeral parlor. He told me he could remember the names of the deceased but not the survivors, and yet the survivors are the ones who pay the bills!

3. Can you make the name sound like a meaningful phrase?
This is similar to number 2, but here you break the name into more than one word and create a phrase with it.

For example, Viner could become "Fine her." Weinstein could become "wine" from a "stein." Gudlauggsen sounds like "good luck, son." Macmeyer might be "muck 'n' mire." Threllkeld can become "thrill-killed."

4. Can you translate a foreign name into its English equivalent?
If your native tongue is English, it's a lot easier remembering the English translations of foreign names because they can often give you clear visual images. Morgenstern is "morning star," Schwartzkopf is "black head," Frias is "cold," and Corazon is "heart."

When substituting words for names or parts of names, don't be worried that you will slip and accidentally call the person by the mentally altered moniker rather than the correct name. If you put the information into your mental computer correctly, the correct information will print out. The important point is to tell yourself clearly *why and how* you are altering the name. At the moment you change the name from something new to something known, consciously lock in the mental association. Both steps are important: create the mnemonic connection and tell yourself what alteration you made to come up with it.

LINK

First names should also be categorized and substituted when possible just as you do with surnames. Here is a list of common names that will get you started. Devise your own categories and substitutions if you think of ones that have more meaning to you or that spring to mind more quickly than these.

PEOPLE NAMED:	ARE:
John	Popes and kings (or like to read a lot privately)
Mary	Merry and ready to marry
Bobby	English policemen
Rose	Sweet or thorny
Robert	Robbers
Bruce	Bruised easily
Virginia	Virgins
Louise	Loose
Bill	Good for paying the bill
Dan	Dandy
Candy	Easy to swallow
Howard	My, how weird
Fred	Ahead
Kate	Good on a date
Julia	Jewels
Arthur	Authors
Elizabeth	Queens
Tom	Tomcats
Ethel	Gassed
Frank	Frank

PEOPLE NAMED:	ARE:
Preston	Pressed upon
Ken	Keen and can
Dorothy	Off to see the Wizard
Joe	Cool
Jim	Jungle Jim gymnasts
Erwin	Urged to win
Marvin	Marvelous
Diane	Princesses or huntresses
Jack	Loaded
Richard	More loaded, they're richer

Always try to link the person's first name to the last name with any mnemonic connection that seems appropriate. Howard Weinstein can become "How weird . . . wine from a stein!" My own name, Hermine, rhymes with 'keen' and is pronounced "her mean" (it's French for ermine) and my last name is an obvious brand name. You can remember my name by thinking: She taught "her mean" memory course in the "Hilton" conference center.

Here are a few examples of first and last name linking:

Arthur Pine	He "authored" a book on "pine" trees.
Mary Street	She lives on a "merry street."
Tom Gray	A "gray" "tomcat."
Carol Antone	She sings a "carol" in San "Antone."
Sharon Ware	She's always "sharin' " her "wares."
Ken Brigham	He "can" "bring home" the ham.
Bill Brewster	You can "bill" me for "stirring the brew."

Philip Berry	"Fill up" the basket with "berries."
Terry Butler	The "butler" will give you a "terry" cloth towel.
Harvey Heydoset	"However" "he does it" it's all right with me.

APPLY

In my seminars I like to let the participants see how easy it is to remember new names by practicing on the people present. First we have the person pronounce his or her name, and we make sure we understand exactly what is being pronounced. We all pay attention to the name we hear as well as the face we see. Upon hearing the name, we immediately throw it into a category, such as names of old friends, names of celebrities, names that rhyme with something, names that represent a color, quality, emotion, or occupation, or names that sound like other words or phrases.

After categorizing, we look to see if there is any natural connection between the person's face and the name, or between the physical frame and the name. If there is, we make good use of it, but in general a person's face or frame do not readily connect with the name.

It's always a good idea after hearing the name to focus on any prominent feature or features you observe in the person. This gets your visual and auditory senses working together toward creating a memorable image. Unfortunately, not all people have prominent features.

If necessary, we do a bit of mental imagineering with the features or mannerisms in order to construct a connection that will lock in the name, but usually just giving the name a relevant meaning while we are engaged in meeting the person is sufficient. If we do care to construct an otherwise nonexistent connection, we don't make it grotesque or distortive. The bizarre connections are the more difficult ones to reclaim upon meeting the same person at a later date.

The next step is to create a related connection between the thought that the name has brought to our minds and the person. For example, we can always tell ourselves a little story about the person using the name we have heard, even though it may be far from the truth, such as "Mr. Ball plays ball," or "Mr. Carson is Johnny's brother," "Miss Antone is a San Antonian," or "Miss Morgenstern will be a star in the morning."

Sometimes we discover a link between the person and name that fits easily into a rhyme. For example:

Mrs. Keating is a hostess, therefore "Mrs. Keating does the seating."

Mr. Pinner is a lean man, and a dance instructor, therefore "He's thin as a 'pin' but big with a 'jig.' "

Here are some other examples of how we have connected the name with the person:

Mr. Eason in radio: He is "easy" to listen to.

Mr. Westmoreland, who works in Arizona: He works out "west" because there is "more land" there.

Mr. Fred Hills, editor at Simon and Schuster: "Fred" gets "ahead" and climbs "hills" to get to work at S&S.

Mr. Daniel Tannenbaum is a very large man and very generous: Translate Tannenbaum to Christmas tree (German) and think of "Big Dan," as tall as a "Christmas tree."

I find at my seminars that, even with a lot of people participating, everyone usually remembers scores of names with these techniques, even after the entire audience changes seats. We must realize, however, that we are not about to be handed connections on a silver platter. We must depend upon our own creative ingenuity to bring home the name.

You can begin practicing this technique immediately. Don't wait until you meet someone new. Simply take your company directory or phone book and run down the list of names, creating mnemonic associations even for people you already know. In fact, previewing a list of names of people you are going to meet is an excellent way to get a jump on the old memory game. If you can walk into a meeting with the names of new people already associated in your mind, then all you'll have to do at the time is link them up with faces and personalities. Similarly, after meeting new people or at the end of a day of introductions, run quickly over each name and face and mnemonic connection, giving yourself suggestions that you will remember the next time you meet.

CONCLUSION

The more you make mental connections between first and last names by categorizing and substituting, the easier it will become. I know countless business people who meet new faces and learn new names each week, and creating these sentences and phrases has become almost second nature to them. In fact, I'd wager that once you begin this process you won't be able to meet a new person without automatically locking in his or her name with mnemonic associations like these. It becomes habit-forming.

5

Counting on Your Memory

Numbers are boring, and there's the rub.

SCENARIO

You step into a phone booth in the airport terminal, your eye on the clock on the far wall. Your plane is due to depart in ten minutes and boarding has already begun. You detest last-minute business details before taking off, but since you had to change your itinerary at the last minute, you know you should alert a new business contact so she doesn't send her report to the wrong city. For some stupid reason, you put her business card in the suitcase that you checked through luggage and there isn't a phone book in the booth.

You dial Information and request the number, asking the operator to repeat it just for good measure. Usually your short-term memory for phone numbers is pretty good. After all, they are only seven digits long, and you don't have to remember them for more than, say, seven seconds. But why take chances?

You deposit the coins, dial the number, and—busy! Damn! You really have to get through. You hang up, swipe your change out of the return slot, redeposit it, and then— you can't believe it! Your mind goes blank! Seven digits down the tube. You're running out of time and patience. You dial the operator again, and (even though it's never happened) you always fear you'll get the same operator, who will recognize you and make some Lily Tomlin-like remark that will make you feel like a dummy. Maybe you could disguise your voice.

THE PROBLEM

Numbers seem to have been designed to prove the Seven-Second Syndrome. We face it all the time. Nobody's safe from it. Furthermore, there seems to be some principle operating that guarantees you will not get better at remembering numbers the more you work with them. In fact, the more numbers that get thrown at you, the more confusing they become. They all look alike.

Yes, numbers seem designed to be forgotten by the human mind. For one thing, they have no sensory quality. They don't appeal to any of the five senses. They don't stimulate the imagination. They're abstract symbols, and as such they are relatively meaningless unless we give them meaning. In addition to being meaningless, they're rather uninteresting, too. So they have a lot working against them.

Not being able to remember phone numbers, addresses, car license numbers, Social Security numbers, and others that we use regularly in our businesses is both aggravating and stressful. No one enjoys having to reach for the phone book yet again, and I've watched executives flick the cards in their Rolodexes as though their memories resided in their index fingers. A lot of time each day is wasted looking up numbers, forgetting them, and looking them up again. Many people on a busy day will put off returning a call unless the number is written on the message. Psychologically, it seems to take up too much time to have to stop and look it up. Each time we forget a number we thought we knew by heart, it reinforces the notion that we have "bad" memories. It creates a defeatist attitude. Like joking about poor memories, forgetting numbers sends a mental suggestion to the unconscious that we *can't* remember them, and the suggestion becomes self-fulfilling. We literally program ourselves to forget phone numbers immediately after we dial them.

THE SOLUTION

The solution is to put meaning into numbers to make them memorable. Since numbers do not convey ideas or create pictures for the mind to visualize, we must do it for them. Since the mind's ear must hear something meaningful if we are to remember it, and numbers are sound without meaning, we must create the meaning. Now there are two ways to create meaning in numbers: either through internal *patterns* in the numbers themselves or by *mental associations*.

In this chapter we will practice several simple mnemonic techniques for remembering isolated numbers. Later we will learn the more complex Master Mnumeric Code that is used for longer numbers and lists of numbers and numbers that must be remembered in a particular order. Furthermore, think of this chapter as practice in overcoming the psychological block that most of us have in thinking that we just aren't good when it comes to numbers. You *can* be good. And for simple isolated numbers, such as phone numbers, addresses, credit-card numbers, lock and safe combinations, and so forth, these basic techniques will be all that you need.

MATHEMATICAL PATTERNS

The most basic pattern in numbers consists of the mathematical relationships that are inherent in the very nature of numbers. For example, in the number 345, we immediately recognize the natural sequence. In a number such as 358, we can see that 3 + 5 equals 8. Natural progressions like 369 are easily spotted, where each digit is increased by the value of 3. If the number were 36912, you could find the same increase by considering the last two digits as 12 instead of 1 and 2. Square numbers are also easy to spot, such as 36, 81, 9, 416 (4 and 16), etc.

Another way to break a long number down into more manageable units is to split it into its two-digit parts. For example, the last four digits in a phone number can be thought of as two double-digit figures. When an operator spits a phone number at you such as 858-2519, most of us would probably find it easier to remember 25 and 19 rather than 2-5-1-9. Two numbers are easier to remember than four, and there is less chance of transposing them. The same method can be used to remember license-plate numbers. S2646-8, for instance, can be broken into S, 26, 46, and 8. You might remember 8 at the end by thinking of it as the next digit in the sequence that could be created by mentally highlighting the 2, 4, 6.

Practice these methods on some long numbers that are important to you, such as your credit-card number, auto-license number, bank-card number, Social Security number, etc. Write each down and study it for any combination, progression, or mathematical relationship that will make the number easier to remember.

MENTAL ASSOCIATIONS

There are several ways to create meaning in numbers by linking them to more familiar associations. I'll show you several methods and let you choose the ones you find most useful. If you understand all of them, you can use the one that will work best on any given number.

First, try *phonetic substitutions*. Prick up your mind's ear and repeat out loud the digits 0 through 10. Listen and you'll hear words such as these:

DIGIT	NAME	SUBSTITUTE WORD
0	zero	oh (also nothing, naught, and love, if you're a tennis buff)
1	one	won, wan
2	two	too, to
3	three	free, fee
4	four	for, fore, (be)fore, etc.
5	five	thrive
6	six	sex, sacks, sax
7	seven	sever, severin', servin', savin', Steven
8	eight	ate, eat
9	nine	nein (German for *no;* we've all heard it in the movies)
10	ten	tan, tin

You can also create phonetic substitutes for double-digit figures, but you'll have to be a little more imaginative. Here are some suggestions, but ultimately you should create your own because it's usually easier to remember something you've devised yourself:

22	two-two	tutu
40	forty	for tea
52	fifty-two	thrifty, too
67	sixty-seven	sexy heaven
93	ninety-three	nine eat free

Use these as models and create others of your own.

Another simple way to give some numbers meaning is to think of them as *famous numbers.* Through tradition and common usage, certain numbers have acquired very clear-cut associations. When you see a famous number either by itself or as part of a longer number, use the familiar association as the mnemonic trigger to remember it. Here is a list of some numbers and the associations usually connected with them:

5—nickel	21—age of consent
6—sexy	24—hours a day
7—lucky	25—a quarter
10—dime	29—hard year
12—months	30—over 30
13—unlucky	31—flavors
16—sweet	52—weeks
19—last year of teens	88—keys
20—20-20 vision	365—days a year

Using famous numbers, you could remember the height of Mt. Fuji as 12,388 feet by thinking of yourself practicing the piano 12 months a year, 3 times a day, until the 88 keys were worn out.

A similar strategy is to look for *famous dates*. For example, the last four digits of some phone numbers are specific years such as 1486, 1935, 1023, 1192, etc. Of course, these particular dates may mean nothing to you, but if they were:

1492   (Columbus reached the Americas)
1941   (America entered World War II)
1066   (the battle of Hastings)
1776   (American independence)

and so forth, you'd remember them rather easily. In any long multidigit number, look for famous dates and use the historical event as a mnemonic connection.

Another way to remember numbers is to convert them into dollars and cents. For example, 1269 could be $12.69 and 30122 could be $301.22. It may not seem to you that there is much difference between remembering a number as a number and remembering it as money, but believe me, there is. Money is more important to us than figures, and numbers expressed as money stick in our memories longer than isolated numbers. Try it the next time you have to remember an address. Instead of, say, memorizing 5589 Spruce Street, think of it as $55.89. You might add a connective thought to the street name and imagine that spruce trees cost $55.89 apiece.

In your personal life there are undoubtedly *special numbers, dates, and years* that have particular meaning for you. Your birthday, wedding anniversary, number of children, spouse's birthday, graduation date, childhood address (that you'll never forget!), the age you did this or that. Incorporate these memories into longer numbers when appropriate, and you'll find the numbers much easier to remember.

For example, if you had to remember an address such as:

2491 Main Street, Apt. 4-D

you might have associations such as:

24, the age you got married
91 as 9/1, September 1st, your mother's birthday
4, the number of children you have.

Then by remembering

"wedding," "mother's birthday," and "kids"

you'd have memorized the address.

Lastly, *rhyming* may help you remember certain numbers. Rhythm and rhyme are very helpful mnemonic devices that always appeal to the imagination. Think, for example, of how many commercials you remember because they have unique or clever rhythms or rhymes. Good copywriters build mnemonic connections into their advertising copy to help the consumer remember product brands. Here are some possible rhyme schemes that you might adapt.

You want to remember a court date:

"Court date, February 8,
Don't be late for the magistrate."

You have to get an important letter out by the 3rd of next month:

"Send a word, by the 3rd."

You want to remember that April 5th the children are coming for a visit:

"The twins arrive, April 5."

You want to remember the office party is November 1st:

"We'll have fun, November 1."

To remember a birthday June 2:

"Baby beckoned, June the 2nd."

To remember the year that Efrem Zimbalist's wife was born:

"On a night at the Met, 1884,
Alma Gluck opened her door."

A relative's birthday:

"December 12th, 1907,
My great grandfather came from heaven."

An historic year:

"Panic, panic, panic time, back in 1929."

And my anniversary:

"Beware the couple full of starch,
Who married on the ides of March."

Using any combination of these mnemonic techniques—mathematical patterns, phonetic substitutes, famous dates, famous numbers, personally significant numbers, and rhythm and rhyme—devise an imaginative way to remember your business address and phone number. I've found that many times when I meet people who are interested in what I do and want to contact me, giving them my own personal code for remembering my address and phone number is better than handing them a business card, which they might lose or throw away. I do them one better. I fix it in their memories so they can't forget me. Here's how it goes:

Hilton Memory
Post Office Box 241499
Los Angeles, CA 90024

(213) 824-3333

First I tell them to remember my post-office-box number by thinking of a "two-for-one" (2-4-1) sale where every item is $4.99. Then for the zip code, I tell them to start with the 9 that concluded the post-office-box number and say to themselves, "Oh, oh—what are the last two digits?" The "oh, oh" represents the two zeros, and the answer to what are the last two digits is "the same as the first two digits," that is, 2 and 4—the same two digits that began the post-office-box number.

As for my phone number, I tell them to use the arithmetical relationship they see in the Los Angeles area code: $2 + 1 = 3$, or 213. To remember the number itself, I suggest they think about the 8 work hours in a 24 hourday, after which they are "free, free, free, free." "Free" is the phonetic substitute for 3.

Putting it all together, anyone can remember how to reach me by saying:

"Two-for-one" sale, $4.99.
Start with the 9.
Oh, oh, what are the last two digits? (24).

2 plus 1 equals 3.
8 working hours in 24
And I'm home free, free, free, free.

CONCLUSION

You might think these are curious connections, but they work. I continue to get letters from people all over the country excited to tell me they remember my address and phone number weeks, months, even a year after they learned it. But it doesn't surprise me in the least. After all, the system works. Take a few seconds to make a conscious and imaginative connection for each of the numbers, and they will lock into your memory for easy recall later.

Work out a mnemonic system for remembering your own address and phone number. Make it clever and simple to explain so that the next time someone asks how to reach you, you can demonstrate how easy it is to remember the information whether you give out a business card or not.

Before going on to the next chapter, consider the following six examples I've worked out using a variety of the techniques presented here. Alternative patterns and mental associations may occur to you as more logical than the ones I've devised. If they do, it means you're already on the road to making numbers memorable.

SOCIAL SECURITY CARDS

822-43-0086

8   2   2   4   3   0   0   86
(I) ate too too (much) for free oh oh (I'm) 86ed

562-40-1999

5   6   2   40   1   999
(I'll) thrive (on) sex too (at) 40 - (I) won 999 (times)

711-40-8312

711   40   8 31   2
(At the) 711 (store) for tea - (I) ate 31 flavors too

CREDIT CARDS

5262-1000-2321-1016

52   62   1000 2   3   21   10
(At) 52 (or) 62 (I'd give) $1000 to (be) free, 21, (or) tan
        16
(and) 16

9900-1010-4400-4973

9   9   0   0   10   10   4   400 49
Nein nein oh oh (Rin) Tin Tin - For 400 49ers
    7   3
heaven's free

0213-1225-1969-1500

0   213   1225   1969
Oh, (I'll call) L.A. (on) Xmas (to talk to) the first man on
                                        1500
the moon (because he owes me) $15 hundred

Tired of reaching into your wallet every time you need to
know your Social Security or credit-card number? Why not
stop right now and create mnemonic connections for the
real thing?

6

Spell It Right

There are worse sins in the world,
but why look like a dope?

SCENARIO

Your secretary is on maternity leave and the temporary help isn't a great speller, but then neither are you. She's made some rather serious mistakes already that went beyond spelling, like typing up letters to the right people but addressing them to the wrong companies. But you don't want to make a big deal of it. You hired the temp as a favor for a friend. Nevertheless, each day she's in the office you can feel the tension build as you begin to distrust her skills. Still, you don't want to let her go. It's only for a few more weeks.

But you don't have time to proofread everything she types, and when there's a stack of letters that need your signature at the end of the day and you're already late for dinner—what do you do? Sign them? Misspelled words are common human errors. Everyone misspells a word now and then, right?

73

THE PROBLEM

The English language is a nightmare. Be glad it's your native language, if it is. While there are plenty of rules governing spelling and pronunciation, it seems there are more exceptions to the rules than cases that follow them. In the family of human languages, English is a real prodigal. Pronunciation is no great help as a clue to spelling, either. We know there are silent *p*'s, *k*'s, *m*'s, *e*'s, and then those weird little trios like *they're, there,* and *their,* and *too, two,* and *to.* Face it, spelling English correctly is no easy matter.

Many executives have told me they gave up in phonics class back in grade school when they decided there were more important things in life than "*i* before *e.*" That independent spirit is probably what makes them good executives. And there are more important things in business than "*i* before *e*" but, as is often said about so many jobs, someone has to do it. It doesn't *have* to be you, but there will be times when it *will* be you. And, as you know, *you* are responsible for all the material that leaves your office. Even the executive I met several years ago who announced defiantly, "I don't care if I go to my grave misspelling 'hieroglyphics,' " would probably be rather upset if he misspelled the name of a client's company, or if an expensive printing job had to be redone because of one small spelling error.

And spelling problems occur regardless of intelligence or level of education. Even brilliant people misspell words and have mental blocks about everyday words or the correct spelling of certain bugaboo words. Writers, too, can list dozens of words they consistently misspell but can get away with if they have sharp copy editors to rely on. For many people, learning to spell correctly is an interest problem not a "smarts" problem, and for many of us (secretaries and stenographers are the exceptions) spelling does not rank very high on our interest scale.

What's more, most of us aren't very good at doing two things at once: and writing and spelling, although they look like the same activity, are really two distinct ones. When we are writing, our attention is focused on composing, shifting ideas, coming up with the right words and phrases. Spelling is secondary. By force of habit we manage to write and spell most of the words correctly, but the uncommon words or difficult words can easily slip in misspelled; especially when we're tired or have a lot on our minds. Remember this, and get in the habit of proofreading what you write *after* it's written. Do this consciously. Often proofreading slips into mere reading, that is, reading for sense, wit, insight, rather than looking for misspelled words. Unless the mind is well focused on the proofing, your eye may *see* the misspelled words but your mind won't register them as incorrect.

THE SOLUTION

Obviously, the solution is a combination of common sense and mnemonics.

First the common sense. Be careful. Many misspellings are due to carelessness because we go too fast and don't take time to proofread.

Next the mnemonics. Recall what we've learned so far. The eye does not do the learning. The mind learns. Rely on the eye alone and you can forget the correct spelling by the time you close the dictionary. Furthermore, you can't rely on the ear for the correct spelling of many English words because the rules of pronunciation have too many exceptions. Remember this sentence: "They're two menie eggs-epshuns." What's needed is a strong connection to assist the mind at the time you are learning the correct spelling. A connection between the spelling and the meaning of the word itself can be a powerful mnemonic association to lock in the correct spelling so you can dredge it up when a dictionary isn't handy. Or look for a connection between the spelling and etymology of the word. Often the root from which the word derives will hold a clue to its spelling.

Here are some examples of how to create mnemonics for commonly misspelled words:

1. There is a BALL in *ball*oon.
2. Don't make an ASS out of yourself on any occa*s*ion, even at a fiesta where CC Señor will serve to remind you of the two *c*'s and the one *s*.
3. You can't take a CAR to the *Caribb*ean but you can take a BB gun.
4. You can't put a DENT in indepen*dent* person.
5. There is always $ involved in an expen$e.
6. Our PAL the princi*pal*. PeoPLE have princi*ple*s and princi*ple*.
7. You can't dance in the DEN and catch up on corre-spon*den*ce at the same time.
8. Don't MAR your gram*mar*.
9. We need an a*ccomm*odation for 2 Children and 2 Mommies.
10. The *im*portant M in Memory is also in *M*nemonic.

CONCLUSION

Once you've created a mnemonic for the spelling of a diffi-cult or "stubborn" word, you won't ever be unsure again.

I've found that the words that I have mnemonics for never give me trouble, but ones that I haven't locked in with a strong mnemonic connection can always make me feel unsure, especially if I think about them too much and simply try to "see" which spelling looks correct. Your eyes can play tricks on you, as I'm sure you know. This further proves to me the reliability of conscious mental connecting over mechanical repetition.

Here is a list of some commonly misspelled business words. Create a mnemonic connection for each of them and you'll never have to worry about spelling them correctly. On the other hand, if you simply memorize them by rote, I guarantee there will be times when you'll be stumped.

misspelled	I don't want to MISS one word.
account	So small you could measure it in CC's.
amount	A pile of money can MOUNT up.
achievement	_____
advantageous	_____
advisable	Wearing SABLE is always adviSABLE.
ascertain	_____
capacity	_____
changeable	_____
clientele	_____
communication	Mass Media.
descent	_____
eligible	_____
existence	Out of exisTENce for TEN years.
guarantee	_____

indispensable   _____

irresistible   _____

knowledge   KnowlEDGE gives us an
                       EDGE.

necessary   _____

noticeable   _____

occur   _____

occurred   _____

permissible   _____

personal   _____

personnel   _____

questionnaire   The Not Nice question Always
                       raises my IRE.

recommend   _____

referred   RefERRed in ERRor.

rescind   _____

rhetorical   A RHetorical RHode Islander
                       tried to RHyme RHubarb with
                       RHinoceros.

separate   How do you RATE A RAT?
                       SepARATEly.

stationary   The giant dictionARY is
                       stationARY.

stationery   _____.

supersede   _____

tariff   _____

transferred   _____

And finally: There is *no* X in ECSTASY but there *is* SIN in buSINess.

7

Creating and Using a Mental File

If only I knew what I knew!

SCENARIO

You dropped by your health club before an important business luncheon and, as you were checking in, someone behind you mentioned a dynamite new product that you think you should look into since it might be something that production could use. You make a mental note of it.

At lunch you overhear snatches of a conversation at the next table and, from the drift of it, it seems there's an article about a competitor in the latest issue of *U.S. News and World Report*. Your subscription copy always arrives a few days after the magazine appears on the stands, so you decide to pick up a copy today, either on your way back to the office or going home. You make a mental note of it.

Squashed in the elevator going to your floor after lunch, you eavesdrop on someone in accounting discussing a hot tip about a stock you've been interested in. You figure you should call your broker that afternoon and look into it. You make a mental note to do so.

Needless to say, back in your office your attention is distracted for the first hour or two, and when you finally get a breather in the middle of the afternoon you try to remember the three leads that you promised yourself you would look into that day. But you can't recall what they were. You can remember where you heard them, but not what they were. You can even remember making mental notes to yourself so you wouldn't forget. Now where did you file them?

THE PROBLEM

The problem, of course, is that you *didn't* file them. You made mental notes, as everyone does, and left them lying in the mental clutter of your unconscious. It happens to everyone. We make a quick reminder to ourselves to remember something and quickly forget it. Even making an immediate mnemonic connection may not "hold" it in place if the thought occurs to you in the midst of other activities where distractions crowd in and your attention is focused primarily on something more important at the time. Forgetting tips like these is especially easy on a day when you have a great many other things on your mind. Isolated information that comes out of the blue has a way of disappearing equally fast if not locked in with a connection that has longer staying power.

Information that comes in sporadic and unexpected doses cannot be organized into acronyms and acrostics like the daily tasks and errands that you know about in advance. When a hot tip materializes, you want to seize it quickly, and pencil and paper aren't always handy to write yourself a note. What's needed is a surefire filing system for the miscellaneous information that pops up in the course of a day, a filing system that, as the saying goes, is always complete but never finished.

THE SOLUTION

Several years ago I realized that, if each of us had a permanent mental filing system in our minds, it would save us from scrambling around for a new mnemonic connection each time another piece of information came along. So I devised the following mental filing procedure that would always be ready to go whatever the occasion. It isn't difficult to learn or use, but it will require some initial planning.

First, imagine the system as having ten index tabs numbered from 1 to 10. Then give each tab a mnemonic label that seems natural and logical to you. In other words, each file needs a vivid, relevant image that you will have no difficulty recalling at any given moment. You already have some ready-made connections of your own, although you probably haven't thought about them in this way. Some may be from childhood rhymes, stories, or jingles.

Here are the ten I use:

1. I am Number One
2. It takes two to tango
3. Three little pigs
4. Four-leaf clover
5. Five-dollar bill
6. Six-shooter
7. Seven dwarfs
8. Eight ball
9. Cloud nine
10. Ten little Indians

There are many other numerical phrases that may come more spontaneously to you or have greater recall power.

What about the three musketeers on a four-poster bed committing the seven deadly sins with Bo Derek (or whomever you consider to be a 10). You may prefer these because the sexual innuendo is easier and more fun to remember! In fact, any mnemonic association that has a sensuous ring to it may prove easy to recall. It's quite normal and natural for sexual connections to occur in mnemonics just as they do in other contexts. It doesn't matter how you remember, just *that* you remember. In any event, pick the images that you can naturally relate to before you lock them in as index cues. Once they are in place, you should continue to use the same ones so that your mental filing system is consistent from one day to the next.

Before we go further, let's try a little exercise to prove to ourselves that our minds really do work naturally and swiftly with mnemonic connectors. If at this point you are still somewhat unsure of your ability to train your memory (or if your unconscious is still taking the "I have a lousy memory" fixation too seriously), this exercise should make you feel more confident.

First, talk to your mind's ear and your mind's eye. See the ten images and think about them. Hear how they sound. Really lock them in place. Now, without looking at them, match each mnemonic image with the number to which it corresponds even though the sequence that I've given you below is not the usual progression of 1 through 10. Write your image on the line to the right of the number.

Here's the number	What's your cue?
9	_____
3	_____
5	_____

10   _____

4   _____

6   _____

1   _____

7   _____

2   _____

8   _____

Once you have each number and its prompter cue locked into place, you can attach facts, data, and information whenever you need to. Use this simple step-by-step procedure:

First, be aware of the new fact or tip. Reduce it to the minimal pieces of information. Some overheard items contain unnecessary data. For example, you may hear that TWA has $119 flights to San Francisco on Tuesdays through Thursdays. It's a simple piece of information, but not all the bits and pieces of it need be filed. It may be enough for you to remember simply that TWA has cheap fares. You can exclude San Francisco since you know you have to go there anyway, and you may be able to exclude the days since you haven't planned your trip yet. So take the information, strip it down to the necessities, and consciously fix your attention on it with a mental suggestion that you are going to remember it.

Second, at this point create a singular mnemonic connection appropriate for remembering the essentials. Use the techniques we have already learned, such as categories, puns, wordplay, substitution.

Third, lock the information into the first available slot in your file by using the mnemonic label as a connector.

Fourth, to retrieve this information later in the day (and any other tips you picked up), simply run through the file consecutively, and either the number or its prompter cue will bring the point back to mind.

Now that you have the basics, let's look at how all ten slots could be filled on a typical business day. First, we will look at ten tips or pieces of information, strip them down, and create a singular connection for each.

1. Juniper Advertising is opening a branch in Minneapolis.
   Singular connection: Juniper is a June pear. Minneapolis is a mini apple.

2. A new award created for excellence in advertising is the Andy Award.
   Singular connection: Raggedy Ann and Andy.

3. The Rex on Olive Street is listed in a business magazine as the best place for a "power lunch."
   Singular connection: Rex the Wonder Dog drinks martinis with olives.

4. Frontier Airlines has $69 fares to New York.
   Singular connection: In 1669 New York was the frontier.

5. A financial-planning seminar will be held at the Hyatt on the fifth of the month.
   Singular Connection: $5 million should make me feel "high at" the Hyatt!

6. An article you just read indicates that Westwood One is the country's largest producer and distributor of nationally sponsored radio programs. Norm Pattiz is chairman.
   Singular connection: Westwood One sounds like "West was won." Norm Pattiz sounds like "Norm pats his."

7. Deloitte, Haskins, and Sells is the name of an accounting firm that a new client deals with.
   Singular connection: Deloitte sounds like "delight." Haskins sounds like "has been." "What a delight it has been to sell to you."
8. The golf world series is in Akron, Ohio.
   Singular connection: Ohio sounds like "oh how." Akron sounds like "achin'." "Oh, how I'm aching for a game of golf."
9. PacTel is the brand name of a new cellular phone you've just heard advertised.
   Singular connection: PacTel sounds like "pack and tell."
10. Bishop Ranch in Northern California has 8.5 million square feet of premier office space.
    Singular connection: The bishop's office space is as big as a ranch.

If that seems like a lot of information to digest at one time, remember that on a normal day all ten items wouldn't descend upon you at once. But even if they did come, say within an hour, your simple filing system could handle them all and keep them for quick retrieval later. Let's see how that would work.

Take the preceding information in the order it was given and file each tip in its appropriate file using the label you have assigned to it.

No. Cue	Info	Connection to cue
1. I am #1	Juniper Adv. Minneapolis	I'm eating a "June pear" and a "mini apple."

No.	Cue	Info	Connection to cue
2.	Takes 2 to tango	Andy Award Advertising	See an ad showing Raggedy Ann and Andy dancing.
3.	3 little pigs	Rex Lunch Olive Street	3 pigs having martinis (olives) with Wonder Dog Rex over a business lunch.
4.	4-leaf clover	Frontier, $69 to New York	A 4-leaf clover on the frontier is worth $69.
5.	$5 bill	Finance Seminar Hyatt 5th	See yourself trying to get "high" with only $5. Bad financial planning.
6.	6-shooter	Westwood One Norm Pattiz	6-shooters were part of How "West Was Won" and Norm can "Pattiz" holster.
7.	7 dwarfs	Deloitte Haskins, & Sells Acct.	The 7 dwarfs meet with their accountants and "delight" in learning that, although they're "has-beens," the movie still "sells."
8.	8 ball	World Series Golf, Akron	Think of being behind 8 golf balls and "achin' " to win the series.
9.	Cloud 9	PacTel cellular phone	See yourself with your back "pack" on cloud 9 phoning to "tell" a friend.
10.	10 little Indians	Bishop Ranch office space	10 Indians on horseback to N. CA to powwow with the Bishop at his Ranch.

CONCLUSION

Now that you've filed each item, you'll find that if you start at index number 1 and go through your file, you will recall all the points you needed to remember.

For practice, take three or four hot items that you heard today or over the last few days and file them away. Run through them after you have done so and give yourself a strong positive suggestion that you will still be able to pull them out later tonight. You'll be surprised that they will all be there waiting for you just as they would had you written each down and placed it in an office file.

8

Effective Speeches, Presentations, and Negotiations

Fear of forgetting should be forgotten.

SCENARIO

You said you could fill the bill, and now the moment of truth has arrived. When they invited you to be the keynote speaker at the national sales seminar, the program director explicitly said that he hoped you would break their long-running pattern of terrible speeches. Complaints had come in each year that the keynote address was either deadly serious, deadly frivolous, or deadly dull. This year he wanted something alive, a speech that was definitely hard-hitting yet high in entertainment values as well. In other words, he was asking you to knock everybody's socks off.

During the dinner you merely pick at your food because a ferocious case of nerves has established territorial rights in the pit of your stomach and is slowly working its way up to the back of your neck. Fear multiplies with each course. Maybe you should have written your speech out word for word. Maybe you should have memorized it word for word. Maybe you should have written it out *and* memorized it word for word. Maybe you should rehearse it one more time; after all, it's been almost an hour since you ran over it. Maybe you should have added more humor. If you can't remember the humor you did include, can you really rely on thinking up funny things to say on the spur of the moment? Have you got your notes? Maybe you picked up the wrong file and left the one with your notes in your hotel room. Maybe you should excuse yourself and head for the rest room instead of the rostrum.

THE PROBLEM

There are two words for this problem and, if you have ever suffered from it, you don't need to be told what they are: stage fright. Speaking before an audience is always ranked extremely high on those questionnaires that ask "What makes you a nervous wreck?" and "What are your worst fears?" It's one of those elusive fears, often irrational and totally outside your control, for the more you tell yourself that you have nothing to worry about, the worse it gets. The tricks you use to calm yourself merely remind your nerve endings that you've lost it. They are in control. Even the most experienced actors and after-dinner speakers suffer from it on occasion.

And it doesn't happen just on stages. You can get the "butterflies" before giving presentations in meetings. It can strike even in negotiating sessions when the team is relying on you to lay out the points and handle yourself with an air of calm self-assurance.

In all its forms and manifestations, stage fright is simply the fear of forgetting, buttressed by the knowledge that you might make a fool out of yourself, offend others by making inopportune statements, and establish a reputation for being a first-class bore. No wonder we rank it so high on our list of fears and worries!

THE SOLUTION

If the problem is basically one of forgetting, the solution is simply to remember what you want to say. In other words, it's a memory problem, and from what you already know about mnemonics, you know that you are not helpless. You can overcome the often self-fulfilling fear that your mind will go blank. There are techniques to recall what you need to know. You already know some of them.

Presenting material in front of audiences, committees, and meetings, however, involves more than just the mnemonic strategies you've been practicing to remember daily tasks and people's names. Making speeches involves preparation and organization, which, if done properly, can improve recall and give you the self-confidence that will eliminate stage fright.

Here are six important tips for preparing a speech:

1. *Be totally familiar with your material.* Writing it out completely or in part is an excellent method for preparing and should not be confused with *giving* a speech that is written out word for word. You are writing it out for yourself, not for your audience. Use this preparation time to soak up the facts and information. Let your mind play with

the key ideas and examples. Become totally familiar with the content and form. Jot down different ways of saying things. Pretend you are being asked questions about each point and then answer them extemporaneously. Relate the key points of your speech to what you already know and believe. Personalize it by linking what you want to say with your own experiences. Even rather formal speeches should have a strong personal element to them. After all, they asked *you* to give the speech, not someone else.

2. *Do not memorize a speech word for word.* Trying it word for word is not the best way to remember it (or give it). This method intensifies the fear of forgetting, since the entire speech would have to be remembered word for word. Furthermore, most speakers come across better if they create the impression that they are speaking extemporaneously, and that's rather hard to do with a speech memorized "by eye," word for word.

3. *Learn the speech by heart.* Obviously, this is not meant to contradict point number 2. I don't mean to learn it word for word or by rote. Knowing the speech "by heart" means to understand the speech, feel it, identify with it. Make it so much a part of yourself that when you give it you are imparting yourself. We remember what is part of us. If you think of the speech as something outside of you, it will be harder to remember. You may recall how difficult it was in high-school speech class to give a famous speech written by someone else. It's difficult to make somebody else's speech part of yourself. Similarly, memorizing even your own speech by rote will not allow you to digest the meat of it with your mind and feelings.

4. *Organize your material with mnemonic cues* that will act as built-in prompters to remind you of the major points while

you deliver the speech. Take the key ideas in each section
and select a buzzword or phrase for each point. Remember
the buzzwords or phrases by incorporating them into one of
the mnemonic techniques you've practiced so far: acronym,
acrostic, or mental filing system.

Create an acronym or acrostic by using the first letter of
each buzzword. If the sections of the speech must be delivered in a certain order, the acronym or acrostic must reflect
that order. If acronyms and acrostics do not comfortably
work here, use the mental filing system.

If the speech has been well organized beforehand with
mnemonic cues, you will not even need to refer to notes
while giving it.

5. *Interlocking ideas* will help you remember those parts of
the speech that need to be delivered word for word, such as
when quoting someone or reciting a maxim. Basically, to
interlock a direct quote means to find a mnemonic cue in
the last word of one sentence that will trigger the first word
of the next sentence. Here is an example:

> "Management finally saw the light. What was being
> spent on executive travel was unnecessary and exorbitant.
> Since the takeover, the company is showing a much bet-
> ter profit picture."

The last word in the first sentence, "light," connects to
"what" in the following sentence if you mentally substitute
watt for "what." "Exorbitant" connects to "since" by substituting *cents*.

By looking for these interlocking ideas and substitutions,
you'll see ahead of time how the ideas flow, and you'll have
the mnemonic connections to assist your memory during
delivery.

6. *Do not practice the speech too near delivery time.* Unlike the executive in the opening scenario, you should *not* want to escape to the rest room to go over the speech immediately before delivering it. There is too much tension as the hour draws near, and you should be focused on relaxing and enjoying yourself before your performance. The last thing you need to do is create more stress for yourself or induce what I call "podium block." If you run through your speech too near delivery time, you may create mental blocks that will repeat themselves at the same spot during your delivery. The worst time to mentally run through the speech is when you are already on the dais. The best time to practice on the day of a speaking engagement is after you wake up in the morning. Or, in the case of a breakfast speech, practice before going to bed the night before.

A PRACTICE SPEECH

Let's say you have been asked to give a speech to help executives become more proficient speakers. Here are the points you want to include that will help them get their messages across to their audiences:

Appearance
Press kit (excite media)
Target audience (know your audience)
Subject (topical and current)
Circuit (particular companies)
Monetary (know your product's value)
Brochure (general printed information)
Public relations (good will)
Video/audio

Follow-ups
Markets (geographically)
Expertise

Using the first initial of each buzzword, we could create this acrostic:

"A Popular Topical Subject Can Make Business People Vie For My Expertise."

From the same list we could also create this mnemonic, which utilizes both the acronym and acrostic techniques. In this second instance we have used the same buzzwords but changed the order.

Circuit	C	Colossal
Subject	S	Starring
Press kit	P	Parts
Target	T	T
Video/audio	V	V
Follow-ups	F	F
Appearance	A	A
Monetary	M	M
Expertise	E	E
Public relations	P	Probably
Brochure	B	By
Market	M	Mañana

Notice how we combined some of the ideas into the acronym **TV FAME.**

If we wanted to make sure of the order, we would probably have to organize the buzzwords into an acrostic. Remember that we have the option of using alternate buzzwords that convey the same cue to us or even making our buzzwords (or a part thereof) part of the sentence itself.

If you wanted to keep the points listed above in this particular order,

1. Appearance
2. Subject
3. Market
4. Expertise
5. Profile and presentation material
6. Follow-ups

you could do so with the following acrostic sentence:

"A Subject Made Entertaining Produces Followers."

In this acrostic I used the words "subject" and "followers" and changed "video/audio," "brochures," etc. to the heading "Profile and presentation material, thereby employing the letter P rather than V.

Add a few *a*'s and *on*'s here and there to hold the buzzwords together and you might organize your acrostic thusly using all the buzzwords in the sentence:

"It Appears a Subject on the Marketplace Expertly Profiles a Follow-up."

REMEMBERING MAXIMS

A good strong quote can add energy and credibility to your speech. Even though the body of your speech should be delivered extemporaneously, quoted material should be given word for word. Some speakers read maxims from notes, but the general feeling is that doing so reduces credibility. If the quote means so much to you that you want to include it, then it should be one that is already a part of your mental baggage. Being able to speak it trippingly on the tongue convinces your audience that you truly believe in it.

Here's how to memorize a maxim:

First, after choosing the quote, be sure you comprehend its meaning before you begin to memorize it. Put it into your own words, and understand what each part, phrase, or sentence of the quote is saying. Remember, you want to memorize meaning as well as words. Words without meaning are quickly forgotten.

Second, there are always certain buzzwords in a maxim. The most important of these are the first few that start it off. If you can get them to roll off your tongue, the rest will usually follow and you won't mix up your maxim! Select the key buzzwords and lock them in with a mnemonic connector, such as a substitute or related word, a pun, or a clever play on the meaning. Below are some examples of how to do this.

Third, if the maxim has several phrases, interlock the last word or thought from one phrase to the first in the next. You can do this the same way we connected "light" to "what" with *watt,* and "exorbitant" to "since" with *cents.*

Here are some sample maxims and the ways I would use their buzzwords as mnemonics:

"BUSINESS *is like riding a* BICYCLE. *Either you keep* MOVING *or you* FALL *down.*"—Anonymous

In this first quote, picture yourself, Mr./Mrs. "Business," riding a "bicycle." The rest is obvious. Don't keep "moving," and you "fall" down.

"A FRIENDSHIP FOUNDED *on* BUSINESS *is better than a business founded on friendship."*—J. D. Rockefeller

Try thinking of Mr. Rockefeller, the originator of the words, in a "friendly ship" with full steam ahead, "finding" a business. Starting with the thought of a "friendly ship" will prevent you from starting off incorrectly with the second part of the quote and the word "business."

"DEPEND *on the* RABBIT'S FOOT *if you will, but remember, it didn't work for the rabbit."*—R. E. Shay

In this third quote the word "depend" is important to get you off to the right start. Why not change the word "depend" to sound like "deep end" in your mind, which is where the rabbit will be if you've got his foot in your pocket.

You may also want to remember the person to whom the maxim or quote is attributed. Use the same process by finding a mnemonic connection between the person's name and something in the quote itself. Here are two rather similar quotes on originality from very different sources:

"Originality is nothing but judicious imitation."—Voltaire

"Originality is simply a pair of fresh eyes."
—T. W. Higginson

I would make the following connections to remember who said what. Think of Voltaire as being "volt" and "air." Then lock the name into the quote by picturing an "imitation volt" of electricity going through the "air." (Real volts are in wires, not in the air.)

In the second quote, change Higginson to "egg and son." Then picture the "eyes" of two "fresh" eggs on your "son's" plate.

Take the following five maxims and locate the buzzwords and decide how you would lock them in for yourself:

"I believe in luck—how else can you explain the success of those you dislike."—J. Cocteau

"Not failure, but low aim, is crime."—J. R. Lowell

"The only limit to our realization of tomorrow will be our doubts of today."—F. D. R.

"Language is the dress of thought."—S. Johnson

"Logic is the art of going wrong with confidence."
—J. W. Krutch

PRESENTATIONS

How often have you discovered after giving a presentation that you left out an important point? Sometimes those forgotten points can make the difference in persuading your listeners to accept your proposal. Often remembering all the points in a presentation is more important than remembering every line in a speech. The speech will still be a pretty good speech without every point (in fact, most speeches could stand to have a few so-called key points omitted!). But important decisions will be made on the basis of your presentation. It's necessary to include all the persuasive points. Furthermore, a presenter is more convincing if he or she can talk from knowledge, not notes.

The solution to remembering all the points of a presentation is to use the buzzwords from the material and link them to prompter cues in your mental filing system. Begin your presentation at cue number 1 and deliver each point in succession, addressing yourself to all the data you've mentally accumulated around each point before you move on to the next. Not only will you remember each point, but they will be in the order that you decide is the most persuasive.

Let's say you had to give a presentation on a new securities offering and you've arranged the following eight points in this order:

Investment objective
Shares offered
Distributions
Redemption
Purchase price
Risk factor
Management fee
Other expenses

You could file them in the first eight divisions of your mental file as follows:

Promptor cue	Buzzwords	Connective thought
1. I am Number One	*Investment objective*	*I* have an *objective* to earn higher income on my *investment*.

Promptor cue	*Buzzwords*	*Connective thought*
2. Two to tango	*Shares offered*	The *two tango dancers offer* to *share* new steps.
3. Three little pigs	*Distributions*	The *three pigs* aren't greedy. Every three months they'll *distribute* the bacon (dividends).
4. Four-leaf clover	*Redemption*	The luck from finding the *four-leaf clover* brings *redemption*.
5. $5 bill	*Purchase price*	I'll *purchase* a share with my *$5 bill*.
6. Six-shooter	*Risk factor*	If you carry a *six-shooter* you *risk* getting shot.
7. Seven dwarfs	*Management fee*	The *seven dwarfs* get a *fee* for *managing* Snow White's affairs.
8. Eight ball	*Other expenses*	No *other expenses* to put you behind the *eight ball*.

As practice, assume that you are to make a presentation on the key points of your product and you want to secure them in your mental file. What association would you create for each in reference to its position in the file?

1. Innovative (advanced technology)
2. Cost-competitive
3. Learner adaptability (easy to use)
4. Easy to maintain and to be maintained
5. Size (takes less space)
6. Numerous applications
7. Powerful, but uses less energy
8. Portable (lightweight)

9. Durable
10. Color-coordinated

NEGOTIATING

Shrewd negotiators can go with the flow of a meeting and not lose control of their facts and figures. This does not mean that they necessarily control the session. It means they can ride the waves, often stirred up by others, without getting swamped. It's a mark of weakness to be too dependent upon notes and written data. You need to keep your mind clear to see where the discussion is going and to counter others' objections.

Often you may not be able to influence the order of the agenda, so you should use an acronym or acrostic rather than your mental file, which would lock you into a certain order that you may not be able to adhere to. Keep the acronym or acrostic clearly in mind, and be aware of the total number of initials that correspond to the number of your points. As the session proceeds, you can mentally erase each letter or word in your mnemonic as you make that point. When you have erased the entire mnemonic from your mental chalkboard, you'll know that you haven't forgotten any key points.

For example, let's say you are negotiating a new contract and the following points need to be clarified:

Travel
Insurance
Marketing
Expenses
Risk

The acronym TIMER would give you the first letter of each point. If, as an afterthought, you wanted to ask about

Time limits
Control

you could add TLC (the acronym for "tender loving care"), which would stand for "time limits" and "control."

If you had these same points and wanted to add a few more, you should move to an acrostic. Let's say you had to negotiate the following points:

Money (Income, Expenses)
Control
Time limits
Risk
Percentages
Office facilities
Travel
Insurance
Marketing
Lecturing

By rearranging the items and using the first letter of each, you could create the following sentence:

Personally	P	Percentages
I	I	Insurance
Love	L	Lecturing
To	T	Travel
Make	M	Marketing
Money,	M	Money
Tons	T	Time limits
Of	O	Office facilities

Ready	R	Risk
Cash	C	Control

For practice, take the following items as key points for leasing an office or warehouse and create a simple mnemonic to help you remember them in the negotiations:

1. Terms of lease (how much? how long?)
2. Option to renew
3. Payments (how and where to be made?)
4. Starting date of lease
5. Deposit arrangements (first and last month)
6. Square footage
7. What is included (carpets, drapes, fixtures, etc.)
8. Rights of lessee and lessor regarding disputes
9. Improvements or remodeling
10. Parking rights
11. Insurance
12. Maintenance
13. Security
14. Restricted uses
15. Utilities
16. Taxes

CONCLUSION

Whether giving a speech, a presentation, or negotiating a new contract, keep in mind the importance of your preparation. Know your material so that you can deliver it "by heart" not "word for word." Organize the buzzwords mnemonically, interlock ideas, and don't rehearse too near delivery time. Your mental notes will assure you that *fear of forgetting will be forgotten.*

9

Digest Some French and Other Foreign Words and Phrases

How do you say "How much is it?" in Swahili?

SCENARIO

You've been hosting Pierre and Denise from the Paris office since Monday, and the week has been a whirlwind of intense business meetings, plant inspections, and heavy socializing. Now that their visit to the States is drawing to a close, you can breathe more easily. Except for Friday evening. To celebrate the conclusion of a successful week, you have made reservations for a special farewell dinner at a luxurious French restaurant. Usually you feel uncomfortable in French restaurants because, for some silly reason, French menu items just won't stick in your head and you've often made a fool of yourself in front of intimidating French waiters. You just don't want to have to ask about the *haricots verts* to be told they're nothing but green beans. And you always pass up the *tête de veau* because it might really turn out to be what it says and, looking around, you notice no one else in the restaurant seems to have a calf's head sitting on his plate. The last thing you want is to make a *faux pas* with French visitors.

But why is it, you wonder, that you have such a mental block with foreign phrases? Your company is doing more and more business in Europe and South America every year. You know that it's important to have at least a smattering of French and Spanish at your command. Yet every time you sit down to order from a French menu, you panic and order *coq au vin* because it's what you always order.

THE PROBLEM

The problem is not that you had more interesting things to do in high school than memorize foreign vocabulary and irregular-verb endings in French or Spanish. You *did*, of course, have more interesting things to do, and you did them. And they *were* more interesting. But the problem probably does stretch back to your school days, where you got the erroneous idea that learning a foreign language meant somehow impersonating a sponge and soaking it up by repeating foreign words and phrases over and over. Most of us didn't *learn* a foreign language in high school precisely because repetition and learning are two different things. All that soaking up didn't even stick! Would you try to increase your English vocabulary by looking at words in a dictionary and simply reading their meanings over and over? To increase your vocabulary requires *understanding* both what the word means and how it is used.

Learning a foreign language, or at least key words and phrases of a foreign language, is important for many executives today. The economies of the world are becoming increasingly interconnected with international corporations dominating entire segments of the global economy. Even on the local level, foreign representatives visit us seeking to do business in America, and we in turn find ourselves traveling to other countries to open branches or discover investment opportunities. Whether it means being able to find your way out of the subway in Tokyo, write a correct business letter to Caracas, skim the lead articles in a German business weekly, or entertain a Parisian delegation at a French restaurant, the modern executive should be able to demonstrate at least a basic knowledge of foreign languages.

Keep in mind that any new vocabulary, whether English or foreign, should be learned in the same way you learn any new information. Mental connections must be made from the new to the known. Simply storing definitions, pronunciations, and translations in your head isn't enough. You must be able to retrieve them when needed and know how to use them. If you've been stumped and socially embarrassed by not being able to pull out the right foreign phrase or word, it's probably because, when you first heard or read it, you missed your mnemonic connection.

THE SOLUTION

Despite your negative memories of Spanish 101, learning a foreign language can be easy and enjoyable. Once you have the motivation to learn a new language, it's simply a process of connecting the new foreign vocabulary to words in your own language. If you already know one foreign language, a second is usually not very hard. Many words are similar in several languages. But even with only your native tongue as a starter, you'll find that there is no word, foreign or native, that can't make you think of another if you put your mind to it.

Therefore, let's begin with an example or two in English. Often the connection between what a word sounds like and its definition proves to be a reliable memory link. For example, the word *sarcophagus* means stone coffin. As I listen closely to the parts of the word, I hear "sorry," "coffin," and "Gus." Putting these words together in a sentence, I have *"Sorry you're in the coffin, Gus,"* and that idea has always brought back the definition.

Nefarious means wicked or traitorous. Listening to the sounds, I hear "no," "fair," and "us." Wicked or traitorous people, like Benedict Arnold, are *"no fair on us."*

My daughter Espreé began remembering words by mnemonics when she was four. I called her "rambunctious" once, and she asked me what it meant. Teasingly, I said it meant the same as "boisterous," which I knew she wouldn't understand. Together we figured out that "rambunctious" sounded like *"ran and bumped us."* The excited cat ran and bumped us! Then she figured out that rambunctious meant the same thing as when her preschool teacher told the girls, "We mustn't let the *boys stir us* up." The sounds of the words and their meaning made a natural mnemonic connection for "boisterous."

We can learn foreign vocabulary in the same "sounds like" manner. Keep in mind that there is no foreign word that won't remind you of one in your native language. To demonstrate this, let's use the numbers one to ten in Japanese, possibly not a language with which you are familiar. Phonetically, the numbers one to ten could be written like this:

1. ichee	6. roh-ku
2. nee	7. shee-chee
3. sahn	8. hah-chee
4. shee	9. ku
5. go	10. ju

Instead of parroting them by rote, let's make up a quick story based on what these words sound like to us in English.

Using the mind's ear, we discover these English words hidden in the Japanese:

One and Two sound like "itchy knee."
Three, Four, and Five sound like "sun, she, go," possibly a sister bay to Montego, named Sanchego Bay.
Six sounds like "row coo," or "row cool" with an *l*.
Seven sounds like "she chea(ts)" if we add *ts*.
Eight sounds like "hot chee(se)" if we add *se*.
Nine and Ten sound like "could you?"

Putting them all together we have a story about a girl who cheats in the sun!

You've got an "itchy knee" to go to "Sanchego" Bay. You'll "row coo(l)" to get there, in order to see a girl whose problem is "she chea(ts)" and eats "hot chee(se)." "Could you?"

Let's review it to see how well it sticks in your mind. Answer these questions without looking for the information above:

What's wrong with your leg?
Itchy to go where?

How will you get there?
What's the girl's problem?
What does she eat?
And you ask yourself?

Moving around the globe, let's try the same with one to ten in French. Spelled phonetically, these numbers read:

1. uhn   6. sees
2. duh   7. sett
3. trwah   8. weet
4. kahtr   9. nuff
5. sanc   10. deess

If you listen closely, you can hear the following sentence:

Un-der (the) *tree* (the) *cat sank, cease*(d), (and) *said, "We-eat* (e)*nuff* (of) *dese."*

You see, it's not as hard as it might sound. Now that you can count from one to ten in Japanese and French, create your own sentence for one to ten in German. Here is the phonetic spelling for it:

1. eye'nss   6. zex
2. tsvigh   7. zeeben
3. dry   8. ahkt
4. feer   9. noin
5. feunf   10. tsain

FREE RELATIVES

In most Western European languages, there are "free" relatives, called cognates, that are so similar to their English counterparts that you can truthfully say that you already know them after the first time you see them. If you can "smoke out" these cognates while learning a new language, you'll be surprised at how many words you already know.

Some cognates are spelled identically to their English equivalents, others come rather close. Look over these Spanish words. I won't even give you their meanings.

tornado	*director*
piano	*canal*
error	*metal*
color	*hospital*
actor	*ideal*
doctor	*rural*
honor	*torpedo*

A third group consists of words whose spellings are not quite the same but whose English meanings are closely related to similar English words. Look over this list carefully just once, and I'll bet you will have 90 percent or more already locked into your memory.

English	*Spanish*	*Connection (reminder word)*
think	*pensar*	pensive
newspaper	*diario*	diary
right	*derecho*	direct
remark	*nota*	note
refuse	*negar*	negate

English	*Spanish*	*Connection (reminder word)*
remember	*recordar*	record
write	*escribir*	scribble
order	*ordenar*	order now
file	*archivo*	archives
book	*libro*	library
list	*lista*	a list
alone	*solitario*	solitude
busy	*ocupado*	occupied
change	*retractación*	retraction
answer	*contestar*	contest
easy	*fácil*	facility
meeting	*asamblea*	assembly
difficult	*difícil*	difficult
mend	*reparar*	repair
chase	*perseguir*	persevere
sell	*vender*	vender
desk	*escritorio*	secretary
lost	*perdido*	perished
drink	*beber*	imbibe
keep	*guardar*	guard
dark	*obscuro*	obscure
high	*alto*	altitude
glad	*contento*	content
finish	*terminar*	terminate
end	*fin*	final

Look for puns, wordplays, and substitutions of similar words (either in sound or meaning) to create mnemonic connections for words that are not true cognates. For example, in Spanish the word for "work" is *trabajar*, which sounds to me a lot like "trouble," which most work often is! In German, the word for "farmer" is *Bauer*, which sounds

like "bower" and that reminds me that a farmer lives in the
bower of nature. And if the farmer is married (*verheiratet*), I
would consider him "very high rated." Use associations like
these for all the new foreign words you need to learn and
you'll find that remembering them is a lot easier than simply memorizing lists of vocabulary by rote. What's more,
you'll assure yourself that you won't "get shafted" doing
business (*Geschäft*) in Germany or anywhere else!

Many cognates differ from their English equivalents only
in their endings. They can be added quickly to your vocabulary with just a little practice in pronunciation. In German
-heit, *-keit*, *-schaft* often take the place of "-hood" and
"-ness" in English. French has similar replacements. Here
are some couplets I wrote as a mnemonic device for myself
before a trip to Venezuela:

> History is to *historia*
> As glory is to *gloria*,
> Dictionary is to *diccionario*
> As necessary is to *necesario*,
> Facility is to *facilidad*
> What ability is to *habilidad*,
> Realism to *realismo*
> Optimism to *optimismo*,
> Perfectly to *perfectamente*
> Usually to *usualmente*,
> Nutrition to *nutrición*
> Condition to *condición*,
> Obsession to *obsesión*
> Possession to *posesión*,
> and Confession to *confesión*.

DIGESTING SOME FRENCH

Let's use some typical items from a French menu to create mnemonic connections for foreign words. Besides learning mnemonics, you'll pick up some French so you'll be able to order with "panache," knowing that refers to style, not pancakes.

First, glance quickly down this list of cognates and impress yourself with how much you could order even now without mishap.

roast beef	*rosbif*
steak	*bifteck*
roast pork	*rôti de porc*
rice	*riz*
radish	*radis*
salad	*salade*
celery	*céleri*
peas	*pois*
spinach	*épinards* (change the *e* to *s*)
asparagus	*asperges*
carrots	*carottes*
olives	*olives*
onions	*oignons*
tomatoes	*tomates*
vinegar	*vinaigre*
tea	*thé*
coffee	*café*
fruit	*fruit*
sugar	*sucre*
cream	*crème*
dessert	*dessert*

cocktail	*cocktail*
whiskey	*whiskey*
gin	*gin*
and, of course,	
cognac is	*cognac*

Next are some French menu items that don't have English cognates but are not difficult to remember using some of the mnemonic techniques we have already learned.

canard, duck
> I think of the English word "canard," which is a hoax. I would always "duck" being part of a hoax.

homard, lobster
> I think of going "home" to eat a lobster.

agneau, lamb
> I think you're a "lamb" because the dinner's "on you." (The *g* is silent.)

côtelettes d'agneau, lamb chops
> I think of "cutlets" as being "chopped" from the lamb.

cuisses de grenouilles, frog legs
> To me this sounds like "green kisses," which I would expect from the handsome prince still in the guise of a frog.

poisson, fish
> This looks like "poison" and I don't want to eat poisoned fish.

jambon, ham
> I hear "hambone."

poulet, chicken
> I think of a "pullet," which is a young hen.

pommes de terre, potatoes

    I think of the *p-d-t* in the French and *p-t-t* in English.

pommes frites, fried potatoes

    Pommes is abbreviated and *frites* is like "fritos." "Mashed" is *en purée*, which you'll understand if you use a blender.

légumes, vegetables

    I think of playing "leg 'ums" (similar to "footsies") under the "table."

champignons, mushrooms

    Not champagne! And because you'd be so surprised to receive a plate of mushrooms if you thought you had ordered a glass of champagne, you'll probably never forget this again. Besides, if you really think hard about it, what do you think champagne is in French??!

pain, bread

    The bread is in the "pan."

beurre, butter

    Butter served on ice is cold—"brrr!"

fromage, cheese

    The cheese is left over "from ma's" supply.

huile, oil

    Use oil to fix a squeaky "wheel."

sel, salt

    The salt is in the salt "cellar."

poivre, pepper

    What can you "pwoove" (with an "ah") by eating pepper?

glace, ice cream

    The ice cream is smooth as "glass."

As far as pronunciation goes, use the solid mnemonic associations to remember the rules of pronunciation in a foreign language or an individual mnemonic for particularly troublesome words and phrases. For example, in French you can "ig*n*ore" the silent *g* before *n* and remember not to get the "D.T.'s" when pronouncing French—that is, don't pronounce the final *d, t,* or *s.* Or remember the sentence "I'm going HOME to see OMAR the tentmaker" for the pronunciation of *homard* (lobster) or "The pullet is POOL-ing your LEg" for *poulet* (chicken).

Not only will you impress your Parisian guests with your knowledge of French, but I'm sure you'll make a big hit with the waiters and waitresses, expecially if you leave a substantial "poor boy"! I don't mean a sandwich. "Poor boy" is my mnemonic for remembering how to pronounce *pourboire.* And any *garçon* will tell you that's a TIP!

CONCLUSION

To sum up, be aware of the foreign word or phrase you want to learn. Check a foreign dictionary for the correct pronunciation and meaning. Be sure you comprehend the meaning. Find the connective "sounds like," cognate, or mnemonic hook to link the new with the known. Last, rethink the mnemonic connection for recall.

10

Master Mnumerics

With the Mnumeric Alphabet you can count on letters
to help you remember numbers.

SCENARIO

You are getting ready for a quarterly sales conference with your company's fifteen regional managers and their top sales people. You glance over the sales statistics from each region and wish you had a way to remember them. You'd like to be able to rattle them off whenever you needed them so you could impress upon the regional people that you take their work seriously and that you don't need printouts to recall what each sales rep did last quarter.

But there's no way you can commit so many similar figures to memory. The simple mnemonic devices you have used successfully for remembering isolated phone numbers or credit-card numbers won't work. So you decide to forget about memorizing all of the stats and just focus on the top three or four. Or should you memorize the worst three or four? It's no use. They all begin to blur into each other.

THE PROBLEM

The problem is being swamped with figures. Figures that are either too long to remember or that come at you in voluminous quantities. As we saw in Chapter 5, numbers in themselves are not inherently memorable, unless they are associated with something else, such as famous dates, your birthday, your age, and so forth. But taken randomly, numbers lack sticking power because they embody no imaginative quality. With a little practice, you might memorize a hundred lines of *Hamlet*. Memorizing a hundred ten-digit numbers, however, would probably drive you berserk.

And yet there are times when you glance over a printout of "meaningless" numbers and wish you could remember a few for future recall. An executive with facts *and figures* at his or her command can argue more persuasively and impress colleagues and clients. What is needed is a reliable, flexible system to remember numbers no matter how complex or how many there are.

THE SOLUTION

The solution is the Master Mnumeric Alphabet—I coined the word *mnumerics*—precisely to answer questions about how to remember long lists of numbers. Executives rank remembering long, complicated numbers along with forgetting names as the most frustrating memory problems they face. Usually, however, people will forgive you for not having *every* figure at your fingertips, but if it is *their* figure you forget, they become less forgiving.

Learning the Mnumeric Alphabet, which we will refer to

with the acronym MA for convenience, is somewhat akin to learning to tie your shoelaces. We all learned how to do that by watching our mothers and fathers do it for us. And that's the way it should be! Imagine how complicated tying your shoelaces would seem if you had to learn it from an instruction sheet (with or without illustrations). Similarly, the MA is more easily learned through a hands-on instructive experience, but in lieu of that you can master it with a little patience from the instructions that follow in this chapter. Bear in mind, however, that it will look more complicated on the printed page than it really is.

However, once you've learned and used the system, you will be totally secure in your ability to capture long figures for recall, even if you have stacks of them. The Mnumeric Alphabet pays off. The time put in up front to understand and employ the system will save hours, even days, of needless repetitive reading later.

THE GROUND RULES

You learned in Chapter 5 that to remember numbers you have to give them some meaning. Mnumerics will give numbers meaning. My definition of mnumerics is "numbers stored through the use of a phonetic alphabet." In other words, we will turn numbers into words by using the Mnumeric Alphabet.

The Mnumeric Alphabet is based on a premise first discovered in the eighteenth century and with which memory experts have been tinkering ever since. It is a simple method of translating numbers into phonetic sounds and using those sounds to form words and phrases.

The MA was devised by assigning a consonant sound from the regular alphabet to each digit from 0 to 9. These sounds are then translated into letters of the alphabet, which are used to construct words or phrases that represent the digits in the original number. I call these words or phrases "translatory" because we get them by translating the numbers into letters. And with these translatory words we can give numbers intelligible meaning and store them far more securely.

Here are the digits 0 to 9 and the letters that represent the phonetic sounds they stand for:

1 = T or D or TH
2 = N
3 = M
4 = R
5 = L
6 = J or G (soft) or SH or CH
7 = K or C (hard) or Q or G (hard)
8 = F or V
9 = P or B
0 = Z or S or C (soft)

(Note: The X sound is a combination of two sounds, K and S, and therefore translates as 70.)

You'll notice that some digits have more than one consonant option, yet each option imparts the same or very similar phonetic sound. In fact, this is one of the reasons that English is such a difficult language to spell. Unless you are specifically listening for the subtle distinctions, it is not easy to "catch" the correct spelling of a word with a K or hard C or Q or even hard G sound. To foreign ears, all these sounds are alike. For purposes of the MA, however, these options are important. They allow us greater variety in the words or phrases we construct to remember numbers.

Note carefully that the vowels A-E-I-O-U have no numerical value in this alphabet, nor do the letters that are already silent in any given word, such as the *k* in "knot" or the first *m* in "mnemonic." Similarly, the sounds made by W, H, and Y ("why") have no value either. To remember these last three, simply ask yourself "why" they have no value. It's a mnemonic in itself.

Next, let's look at a few English words and study their phonetics so we will understand the MA more thoroughly.

The word *phase* has five letters but, phonetically, the ear hears only three. They are: an F sound, a long A, and a Z. It's interesting that the word itself doesn't have an F or a Z!

Now "phase" is a translatory word for the number 80. How so? The F sound stands for 8; the A is a vowel and hence has no numerical value; the Z sound is worth 0; the E, another vowel, has no value.

The word *tough* stands for number 18. The T is 1; O and U are vowels and hence valueless; the GH is an F sound, worth 8 (as in "phase").

One more. The word *night* has the sound of N and T and is the translatory word for 21. I is a vowel; G is silent; H is one of the "W-H-Y" letters that are valueless. Notice that we could also construct other words for 21: "not," "note," "nut," even "knit" and "knight." So you see there are a lot of options for devising translatory words and phrases to help you remember long numbers.

HOW TO REMEMBER THE PHONETIC SOUNDS

You probably guessed that I would suggest a mnemonic strategy to remember these phonetic sounds and the numbers to which they correspond. Here is the one I give in my memory seminars, but if you discover other memory connections that are more natural for you, by all means use them. If you pay attention to each connector cue and the number and sound it joins, you will learn the alphabet very easily. But if you merely try to rote-learn the number and its corresponding sound, I think you'll find it much more difficult and retention will be poor.

No.		Sounds	Connector cue
1	=	T or D	Touch Down—number 1 team. (The *th* sound is also valued as 1.)
2	=	N	N when handwritten has 2 loops.
3	=	M	M when handwritten has 3 loops.
4	=	R	R is the 4th letter in the word *four*.
5	=	L	L is the Roman numeral for 50.
6	=	J, soft G, SH, CH	J resembles a backward 6, and, adding up all the letters shown in this grouping, J-G-SH-CH gives us the sum of 6.
7	=	K, hard C, Q, hard G	The figure 7 is in the handwritten capital K, and K, hard C, and Q are the

No.		Sounds	Connector cue
			same sounds, whereas the hard G is similar.
8	=	F or V	Think "Ford made a V8 engine," F V 8.
9	=	P or B	P is a 9 backward and B is a Pregnant P or Pot Bellied P.
0	=	Z, S or soft C	Zero is spelled with a Z and the sibilant S and soft C, which make the same sound, will naturally follow.

HOW TO USE THE MNUMERIC ALPHABET

To demonstrate how to use the MA, we will translate four phone numbers. The advantage of the MA over the mnemonic techniques we learned in Chapter 5 is that it is much more flexible, allowing you to make significantly different translatory sentences for remembering phone numbers. If you have several numbers to memorize at once, the simpler methods in Chapter 5 will produce rather similar-sounding sentences. The MA, however, gives you more room for creativity.

Let's begin with the number 242-1291.

First, assign a phonetic letter/sound to each of the digits in this number.

2 = N
4 = R
2 = N
1 = T

2 = N
9 = P
1 = D

(Note: we had options with number 1 and 9.)

Second, lay out the sounds/ letters in the order of the digits they represent to create the translatory words/phrases.

N R N T N P D
No ReNT No PaD

Try these numbers:

753-0313

   C L M S M T M
   CaLl Me SoMe TiMe

658-0995

   SH L V S P P L
   SHe LoVeS PeoPLe

590-7327

   L P S C M N G
   heLP iS CoMiNG

In each of these examples, the process is the same. Transpose the numbers to their sound values and look over the letter choices for each digit. Some will have more than one possibility. After deciding which letters to use, insert vowels or the "W-H-Y" letters wherever necessary to make a word. Always try to transpose into letters that will create the most helpful word or phrase for remembering the number and to whom (or what) it belongs. In other words, if your translatory words or phrase can say something relevant about the person who has this phone number, it will be locked more securely into your memory.

Try the following area codes for practice:

Manhattan	-	212
Los Angeles	-	213
Nevada	-	702
South Dakota	-	605

Here are the translatory words I created. See if you can spot the area code within each one:

Cousin
Indian
Shoe sale
No time

The MA can be used for simple numbers, too. Once you've learned it, you may never want to go back to the other mnemonic techniques. With practice you'll automatically think of the phonetic sounds and quickly scan the various letter options. For example, if on a business trip you want to remember Suite 2660 because someone important is staying in it at the hotel, find a translatory phrase for it. You'll know that the number 6 gives you four choices: J, G, SH, CH. In a matter of seconds, you will come up with

Suite 2660 = N CH CH S

out of all the options because you want to construct No CHoo CHooS. Why? The person staying in this suite works for Amtrak!

Use the MA to remember important dates. For example,

the assassination attempt on President Reagan was on March 30, 1981. First, translate the date into 3/30/81. Then scan for the right letters. In this case: M M S F T. A proper phrase to describe his would-be assassin is: hoMe MiSFiT.

How about the following translatory phrase for the stock number of a certain airplane part:

"Fly me home safely please."

If you pick this one apart, eliminating vowels and "W-H-Y" letters, you get

F L M M S F L P L S.

Converting this back into numbers, you have 8533085950, which, when properly grouped, is stock number 8533085–950.

CONCLUSION

One way to practice learning the MA is to transpose numbers and letters on license plates while you are driving to work and home. But you can start right now by flipping through your Rolodex and creating translatory sentences for the phone numbers you use most frequently. Write them on your Rolodex cards and say them to yourself whenever you dial them. Eventually the phrase will unlock the number and you won't have to spin your Rolodex.

I once taught the male inmates in a maximum-security prison how to use the Mnumeric Alphabet. I figured they would use it primarily for examinations in courses they were taking, prison numbers, cell numbers, and so forth. It wasn't long, though, before I realized they had an even more ingenious use for it. Swearing by numbers! It must have worked, because a few months later I received the following letter from them recorded on a cassette:

> Dear Miss Hilton,
> We all passed our examinations with the use of the mnemonic memory training you gave us and we really want to thank you and MA.
> Honestly, Miss Hilton, 261!!

Only the initiated would be able to decipher 261 as "N SHT"!!

11

The Master Mnumeric Code

Say the secret word, and you'll remember everything.

In this chapter you'll discover the important steps for creating a Master Mnumeric Code that will combine the best features of the simple mental file you learned in Chapter 7 with the Mnumeric Alphabet explained in the last chapter. By incorporating the principles of each system into a Master Code, you will expand your capacity to remember large amounts of information with a mnemonic technique that is serviceable, dependable, and as comprehensive as you choose to make it.

In the simple file system, you created mnemonic connections for each index from 1 to 10. These memory cues were somewhat arbitrary in that you either used the ones I suggested ("I'm Number One," "Two to tango," "Three little pigs," etc.), or you figured out your own original cues. Obviously, the system has its limitations in that it would be impossible to come up with mnemonic associations for all numbers from 11 to infinity. Nevertheless, it's a simple, easy-to-use filing strategy when you have a limited number of items to remember.

The Master Mnumeric Code, however, is virtually limitless. Each index is labeled with a mnemonic cue that is logically derived from the Mnumeric Alphabet. Because the system is consistent, it can be extended as far as you can count. We will begin with the first ten slots, learn the code word for each, and practice with them before expanding the system beyond 10.

THE FIRST TEN

The mnemonic cues for the first ten places are:

1. haT		6.	SHoe
2. honey		7.	Cow
3. hoMe		8.	hiVe
4. heRo		9.	aPe
5. hiLl		10.	wooDS

The capitalized letters correspond to the sounds in the Mnumeric Alphabet (see Chapter 10). The other letters in each word are valueless either because they are vowels, or "W-H-Y" letters, or because they are silent. Note that for number 5, even though there are two *l*'s, the ear hears only one. The other is silent.

If you have been using the Mnumeric Alphabet, you are already familiar with these letters. If you are still a bit unsure of yourself, you might find it helpful to incorporate the images from your simple file to make some secondary mental connections for these code words and their respective numerical values to help lock them in at their correct positions.

By visualizing these mnemonic images, the code words will become securely implanted in your mind for future use.

No.	Code word	Mnemonic image
1	haT	You wear the top #1 HAT.
2	hoNey	It takes 2 people to have a HONEY. (Even a narcissist needs a mirror image.)
3	hoMe	3 pigs in the HOME.
4	heRo	4 leaf clover on the HERO's uniform.
5	hiLl	$5 to ride up HILL.
6	SHoe	6 "SHOE-ter."
7	Cow	7 dwarfs milk COW.
8	hiVe	8 ball is beeHIVE.
9	aPe	9-foot APE touches cloud 9.
10	wooDS	10 Indians in WOODS.

Before we proceed, let's test these original ten code words to see how well you remember them. Write in each code word at its respective number. If you run into difficulty, mentally review the visual image that connects the word to the number.

1. _____   6. _____

2. _____   7. _____

3. _____   8. _____

4. _____   9. _____

5. _____   10. _____

Next, test yourself on the words out of sequence. Rethink the sound value or the visual connection, or both, and give back the number.

hero	_____	hat	_____
woods	_____	cow	_____
honey	_____	shoe	_____
home	_____	ape	_____
hill	_____	hive	_____

Now that you have these first ten down pat, any new material that you care to remember can be attached to one of the code words in this master file much the same way you used the prompter cues to store information in your simple mental file.

FILING AWAY THE TOP TEN CEOs

Suppose you wanted to file away the names of the CEOs of the ten largest privately held companies in the country according to their fiscal-year-end rankings. You could do it in a matter of minutes with the Master Mnumeric Code.

To prove the point, let's use the names of the first ten presidents of the United States, who were in fact the CEOs of the national government. Even though you may have drilled these men into your short-term memory in high school, I'd wager that they haven't stayed in place unless you have had reason to use this information over the years. First, we'll put them in their correct order, create mnemonic associations to link them with the Master Code, and then pull them back out in whatever order we wish.

No.	*Code word*	*President*	*Mental connection (auditory and visual)*
1	haT	Washington	You're WASHING your HAT and, wet, it feels like it weighs a TON.
2	hoNey	Adams	ADAM and Eve, the first 2 HONEYs of creation.
3	hoMe	Jefferson	The famous presidential HOME, Monticello, belonged to JEFFERSON. (*Remember Monticello by thinking of a HOME being made out of a MOUND OF JELLO. It's a sound-alike mnemonic.*)
4	heRo	Madison	Picture the HERO being MAD AT HIS SON. Sounds like Madison.
5	hiLl	Monroe	See a long line of MEN IN ONE ROW going up the HILL. Another sound-alike. "Men in one row" sounds like Monroe.
6	SHoe	Quincy Adams	He was the son of the 2nd President, John

No.	Code word	President	Mental connection (auditory and visual)
			Adams. Quincy ADAMS stepped into the SHOE of his father.
7	Cow	Jackson	Prod the COW along in your mind with an "old hickory" stick. "Old Hickory" was JACKSON's nickname.
8	hiVe	Van Buren	Put the HIVE in a moving VAN in your mind. The VAN has BEER ON it.
9	aPe	Harrison	See the big 9-foot-tall hairy APE with his HAIRY SON (Harrison).
10	wooDS	Tyler	Picture a TILE walkway thru the WOODS. This should tick off Tyler in your mind.

Now that the presidents are filed away, you should be able to retrieve their names and their positions in history in whatever order you choose. Take the sequence given below and the code word thrown in to assist you, and write the correct name on the line to the right.

No.	*Code word*	*President*
6	shoe	_____
7	cow	_____
3	home	_____
1	hat	_____
10	woods	_____
9	ape	_____
5	hill	_____
4	hero	_____
2	honey	_____
8	hive	_____

THE MASTER MNUMERIC CODE WORDS

You are now about to embark on a truly mesmerizing venture. With the Mnumeric Alphabet and your understanding of how it spawned the first ten code words, you are about to proceed to set up the Master Mnumeric Code, which will enable you to preserve limitless amounts of information and have it handy for instant recall.

The Master Code, which we'll refer to as the MC, is derived from the MA (Mnumeric Alphabet) with which we can create translatory words for every number from 1 to as high as we care to go. Each code word is derived logically and consistently from the phonetic sounds of the MA, which enables us to keep an index file in our minds at all times ready to receive new information. Since there is no limit to how high we can count, there is no limit to the number of indexed code words we can have in our MC file.

Here are the first fifty to start you off:

1. haT	14. TiRe	27. iNK	40. RoSe
2. hoNey	15. hoTeL	28. kNiFe	41. RaT
3. hoMe	16. DiSH	29. kNoB	42. RaiN
4. heRo	17. DoG	30. MooSe	43. RaM
5. hiLl	18. DoVe	31. MuD	44. waRrioR
6. SHoe	19. TuB	32. MooN	45. RaiL
7. Cow	20. NoSe	33. MoMmy	46. RoaCH
8. hiVe	21. waND	34. haMmeR	47. RuG
9. aPe	22. NuN	35. MuLe	48. RooF
10. wooDS	23. gNoMe	36. MatCH	49. RoPe
11. TiDe	24. New yeaR	37. haMmoCk	50. LaCe
12. TiN	25. NaiL	38. MuFf	
13. TeaM	26. hiNGe	39. MoP	

With these fifty code words from HAT to LACE you have a clear vivid image for each of the fifty numbers. Remember that figures do not stimulate one's imagination. Therefore, it is necessary to convert figures into meaningful or imaginative phrases and sentences. When we recall these phrases or sentences, we have words that can be quickly reconverted into their original numerical values. It's important that these fifty words become a permanent feature in your mental repertoire and as automatic as the ABCs. However, if you ever forget one, it's easy to reconstruct it because you know the original phonetic alphabet (the MA) on which these words are based. For example, if you forget the word for 46, you can reconstruct it by pulling out the R sound for 4 and the J, G, SH, or CH sound (all phonetically similar) that stands for 6. In a few seconds, ROACH should come to mind as the code word for 46.

You can use these fifty code words or create ones of your own. If you decide to substitute your own for any or all of the above, follow these two guidelines:

First, make each code word a strong, concrete noun.

Second, use the exact phonetic sounds from the MA in the words you choose.

THE PRESIDENTS OF THE UNITED STATES: ONCE AND FOR ALL

To practice using the expanded Master Code, let's continue learning the presidents of the United States, keeping in mind that they could be the CEOs of forty famous companies or the names of the top forty sales representatives in your own company. The advantage of using the presidents for practice is that their positions and order are not subject to change, whereas today's sales rep might be tomorrow's CEO, and vice versa.

Here are the numbers from 1 to 40, their code words, and the presidents listed in their proper order:

No.	Code word	President	No.	Code word	President
1.	haT	Washington	13.	TeaM	Fillmore
2.	hoNey	Adams	14.	TiRe	Pierce
3.	hoMe	Jefferson	15.	hoTeL	Buchanan
4.	heRo	Madison	16.	DiSH	Lincoln
5.	hiLl	Monroe	17.	DoG	A. Johnson
6.	SHoe	Quincy Adams	18.	DoVe	Grant
7.	Cow	Jackson	19.	TuB	Hayes
8.	hiVe	Van Buren	20.	NoSe	Garfield
9.	aPe	W. H. Harrison	21.	waND	Arthur
10.	wooDS	Tyler	22.	NuN	Cleveland
11.	TiDe	Polk	23.	gNoMe	B. Harrison
12.	TiN	Taylor	24.	New yeaR	Cleveland

No.	Code word	President	No.	Code word	President
25.	NaiL	McKinley	33.	MoMmy	Truman
26.	hiNGe	T. Roosevelt	34.	haMmeR	Eisenhower
27.	iNK	Taft	35.	MuLe	Kennedy
28.	kNiFe	Wilson	36.	MatCH	L. B. Johnson
29.	kNoB	Harding	37.	haMmoCk	Nixon
30.	MooSe	Coolidge	38.	MuFf	Ford
31.	MuD	Hoover	39.	MoP	Carter
32.	MooN	F. D. Roosevelt	40.	RoSe	Reagan

I'll give you connective hints for some of them and leave the remainder to your own imagination. After all, your personal political leanings, memories, and evaluations of these men will make the connective images sharper and give them greater sticking power.

At 11, you could get POLKed by a fierce TiDe.

At 12, the TAILOR sews the suit for the TiN man.

At 13, the ditch-digging TeaM could FILL-MORE.

At 14, you can PIERCE the TiRe.

At 15, the hoTeL has BLUE CANNON towels.

At 18, peace could be GRANTed to the DoVe.

At 19, the TuB water creates a hot HAZE.

At 20, GARFIELD the cat is NoSe-in' around.

At 22, you just can't get NuN in CLEVELAND,

& 24, not even on the New yeaR.

At 25, McKINLEY was really NaiL-ed.

At 30, the MooSe sat on a COOL LEDGE.

At 31, HOOVES in the MuD.

At 32, ROOSEVELT served for many a MooN.

At 33, a TRUE MAN is true to MoMmy.

At 34, EISENHOWER haMmeR-ed his stars on his uniform.

Why not practice these about fifteen minutes a day while you're driving, showering, jogging, exercising, or otherwise physically engaged. It would be a valuable use of your time. It's good for concentration and will keep your memory exercised also, while testing it at the same time.

USING THE MASTER MNUMERIC CODE TO FILE STATISTICS

As an executive, you may need to remember and compare statistical data from the market in order to measure your own company's gains or losses against market share. You can use the Master Mnumeric Code to lock in statistics such as these. Let's practice with the six savings and loans that *California Business Magazine* ranks among the hundred largest privately held companies in the state. They rank in this order:

No.	Rank	Company	Revenues (millions)
1.	17	Coast Savings and Loan	$692
2.	52	Central Savings and Loan	258
3.	70	Pacific Savings Bank	209
4.	72	Bay View Federal Savings and Loan	207
5.	73	San Francisco Federal Savings and Loan	204
6.	84	Eureka Federal Savings and Loan	169

First, we must translate their numerical ranks and revenues into words. Use any or all of the information in the data to create a visual scene that you will remember.

For example, the first company ranks seventeenth and its revenues are 692. Now we know from our MC that the translatory code word for 17 is DOG. However, we could devise an alternative word that would fit better with other information we are processing. DOG comes from the number 1 being phonetically either a T or a D. The 7 can be represented by K, C, Q, or G. Therefore, we have several possible word choices: DOG, TAG, TIC, DOC, etc. You might want to stick with DOG because you have already memorized that as the permanent code word for 17. On the other hand, if one of the other possibilities offers a sharper image for remembering the specific information, feel free to select another. We'll use TACK.

For the number 692, we have several phonetic options for 6 (J, soft G, SH, or CH) and 9 (P or B), but only the N sound for 2. Possibilities are SHIP IN, CHOPIN, SHOW BAN, SHOPPIN', JAPAN. We'll use SHOPPIN'.

There will be a number of possibilities with each multi-digit figure. It's up to you to create the most workable one in each situation. Sometimes it's like solving a puzzle. When you have many figures to deal with, sit down with pencil and paper and work out the possible translatory words and pick the ones that best tie into the rest of the information. This preliminary organization prior to filing is a most important step. Once the figures are translated into words, create a scenario that will tie together the company name, the translatory words, and the code word where this entry will be filed.

In our example, we are creating a scenario using *COAST* (which is the name of the company) with TACK (which is a translatory word for 17) and SHOPPIN' (a translatory word for 692), and hooking these into the first code word in the master file, which is HAT. Here is what we get:

I'll TACK on my HAT and go SHOPPIN' up the *COAST*.
   (17)   (1)   (692)

Use this same process on the other savings and loan companies, starting with the numbers so you'll know what translatory words you'll have to work with. Here is one way to file them:

No. Code   Co.   Rank   (trans.)Revenues(trans.)
word

1. HAT   Coast   17   TACK   692   SHOPPIN'
   I'll TACK on my HAT and go SHOPPIN' up the *COAST*.

2. HONEY Central   52   LEAN   258   NO LOVE
   Can't LEAN on my HONEY who's in *CENTRAL* America
   so I have NO LOVE.

3. HOME   Pacific   70   GAS   209   NO SOUP
   At HOME we have a GAS stove but there's NO SOUP to
   PACIFY the baby.

4. HERO   Bay View 72   GUN   207   NO SACK
   My HERO has a GUN and a *BAY VIEW* but gets NO
   SACK time.

5. HILL   S.F.   73   COME   204   NO SIR
   Do you want to COME to Nob HILL in *SAN FRANCISCO?*
   NO SIR!

6. SHOE   Eureka   84   FIRE   169   TOUCH UP
   EUREKA! I found my SHOE after the FIRE but it needs a
   TOUCH UP.

For further practice, create other translatory words for the figures in these statistics and then write alternate scenarios for remembering these same six companies.

Now take the next two companies ranked seventh and eighth and put them in your file at 7 and 8 respectively.

No.	Rank	Company	Revenues (millions)
7.	7	Blue Shield of California	$1825
8.	8	Certified Grocers of California	1700

CONCLUSION

If you are wondering, "Do I really have to go through all this?" and "What would I do if I had loads of statistics to learn?," the answer is yes, and with loads of statistics you really have no other options. Unless you're a "wonder kid," I doubt that you'd be able to memorize them by rote. Give yourself time to get the hang of it and practice on reasonable amounts of statistics at first. You'll be amazed at what you can accomplish with your own memory.

12

Remembering Lists

*Organize your mental memo pad and you can forget
the pencil and paper.*

SCENARIO

It's a typical Friday—TGIF, as you used to say back in your
college days before you knew what mnemonics were—and,
as on most Fridays, your time is divided between normal
business responsibilities, professional errands, and personal
chores you hope to get finished before the weekend. In the
morning, before you left for work, you mentally counted
through them and you were appalled to note that there were
ten items on your list: go to the bank; get a license; buy a
magazine; go to the dentist; call your lawyer; buy groceries
(a list in itself!); pick up razor blades; pay the light bill;
take a friend to lunch; buy a gift for your cousin's shower.
And as on most Fridays, you were dead tired when the day
ended and not sure you remembered to do everything.

THE PROBLEM

As we've seen before in earlier chapters, if you don't lock it in, you lose it. Sometimes the harder we try, the less likely we are to remember. The old subconscious plays hide-and-seek with the items on our mental lists. We should know by now that we can't just "figure" on remembering something when the time comes. Even lists that don't seem all that complicated when we make them in the morning can get extremely troublesome by afternoon as we eliminate some items and add new ones that spring up during the course of the day.

THE SOLUTION

At this point in your mnemonic training, you have several options for remembering lists: the basic acronyms, acrostics, the simple file or the Master Code.

For remembering short lists of similar items, such as grocery or shopping lists, the acronym or acrostic is the easiest. For example, if you had to pick up oysters, caviar, Dom Perignon, and shrimp for a party, you could arrange them so their first initials spelled DOCS.

D - Dom Perignon
O - oysters
C - caviar
S - shrimp

If acrostics appeal to you, the same items could be arranged to spell DO COME OVER SOON.

Do	D	-	Dom Perignon
Come	C	-	caviar
Over	O	-	oysters
Soon	S	-	shrimp

If the list was a little longer, you might want to tack the items into the simple mental file of 1 to 10 (number one, two to tango, three little pigs, etc.) Let's suppose that, besides the luxuries for the evening cocktail party, you added a few mundane items:

cookies	cat food
apples	ice cream
vitamins	cereal

Here is how you could plug them into your simple mental file. Be sure to listen to the connections with the mind's ear or visualize them with the mind's eye.

No.	Cue	List item	Connective thought
1.	I am #1	Dom Perignon	*I* am drinking *champagne.*
2.	2 to tango	oysters	*2 oysters* are doing the *tango.*
3.	3 little pigs	caviar	*They* live in a *cave.*
4.	4-leaf clover	shrimp	*4 shrimp* sit on *4-leaf clover.*
5.	$5.00	cookies	*$5.00* for *cookies.*
6.	6-shooter	apples	*Shoot 6 apples* off a tree.
7.	7 dwarfs	vitamins	*Dwarfs* take *vitamins* and grow.
8.	8 ball	cat food	*Cat* is hungry, *licks 8 ball.*
9.	cloud 9	ice cream	*Clouds* look like *vanilla.*
10.	10 little Indians	cereal	*Indians* eat corn *cereal.*

Now suppose that your list of errands is the one presented in the opening scenario. Some of the items you knew about early in the morning; others occurred to you as the day went by. To complicate matters, it's a mixed bag—apples and oranges, as the saying goes, but worse, more like apples and lawyers. In this case, you'd do better starting off the day by putting your errands into the Master Code and adding to it as others pop up.

Just for review, here are the first twenty code words:

1 haT	6 SHoe	11 TiDe	16 DiSH
2 hoNey	7 Cow	12 TiN	17 DoG
3 hoMe	8 hiVe	13 TeaM	18 DoVe
4 heRo	9 aPe	14 TiRe	19 TuB
5 hiLl	10 wooDS	15 hoTeL	20 NoSe

First, line up the errands in the order you need to perform them as far as you can determine. Put each next to the mnumeric code word.

Second, create a mental or visual connection linking each code word to each errand. I've offered some mental associations to give you the idea, but by now you should be getting pretty proficient at this. Lay a piece of paper over the right side of the page to hide my mnemonic associations and devise some of your own. As you do, slide the paper down the page and compare yours with mine.

No.	Cue	List item	Connective thought
1.	haT	Go to the bank	See yourself tossing your big HAT into your bank. The teller catches it and fills it with one-dollar bills.
2.	hoNey	Get a license	Think of you and your HONEY in the act of buying a marriage license at the license bureau.

No.	Cue	List item	Connective thought
3.	hoMe	Buy a magazine	See yourself relaxing in your den at HOME reading a copy of *Business Week*.
4.	heRo	Go to the dentist	Can't you just see your HERO sitting in the dentist's chair? The dentist is working on his teeth to make his smile sparkling white.
5.	hiLl	Call your lawyer	Envision your lawyer delivering an explosive speech to the judge and jury on top of the HILL, winning your case.
6.	SHoe	Get groceries	See the old lady who lived in a SHOE rationing out groceries to each of her children.
7.	Cow	Buy razor blades	See yourself trying to shave the COW.
8.	hiVe	Pay the light bill	Mentally watch a swarm of bees from the HIVE circle a light bulb as it blinks on and off.
9.	aPe	Take friend to lunch	See your friend as an APE eating lunch with you. Everyone is staring.
10.	wooDS	Buy a gift	Picture the WOODS filled with Christmas trees under which are many gifts.

Look the list over until you have each errand and its mnemonic connector locked in place. Then test yourself. Go through the code word file from 1 to 10, connecting each code word to the data filed away there.

1. HAT   What do you see? What's the errand?
2. HONEY   "   "
3. HOME   "   "
4. HERO   "   "
5. HILL   "   "
6. SHOE   "   "
7. COW   "   "
8. HIVE   "   "
9. APE   "   "
10. WOODS   "   "

Now try it backwards from 10 to 1. Here are the code
words backwards.

WOODS
APE
HIVE
COW
SHOE
HILL
HERO
HOME
HONEY
HAT

Last, come up with the errands out of sequence. Look at
the digit. Rethink the code word, and let your image cue
the errand.

2-
5-
7-
10-
4-

1-
6-
9-
3-
8-

Now just when you thought it was safe to think about more pleasant things, five more errands come to mind!

Get a haircut
Place an ad
Order video tapes
Call the plumber
Make a mortgage payment

Lock these five into slots 11 through 15. Then, to get into the practice of replacing your files with new data each day, take these five newcomers and put them in slots 1 through 5. Each time you add a new item to an old slot, you will have to come up with new associations. It won't be hard, however, because the more you work with the basic code words, the more familiar they will become to you and the more quickly you'll be able to plug them into new information.

Here's how I would add these five new errands into the first five slots.

1. Haircut   —You're keeping your HAT on to cover up your long straggly hair.
2. Ad   —Place an ad for a new HONEY in the want-ad column.
3. Video tapes—See yourself at HOME watching a great movie on your video.

4. Plumber   —The plumber patches the leak and is your HERO of the day.

5. Mortgage   —It takes a big mortgage payment to pay for the mansion on the HILL.

CLOCK-WATCHERS

If you think you spend too much time watching the old clock on the wall, let me suggest something different. Forget the clock on the wall and watch the clock in your head! You might still find yourself late for appointments, but at least you'll know whom the appointments are with and what the topics of discussion are. What I'm suggesting is that you convert your Master Code from a filing system to a daily appointment calendar. Here's how it works.

Let the first slot be the first hour of the business day. We'll make that 9:00 A.M. Assume that you're scheduled to meet with Jim Kerrigan, chief executive officer of Trailways. Here's how you could arrange your Master Code:

Time: 9:00
Code word: APE
Name: Jim (Jungle Jim)
             Kerrigan (sounds like "carry gun")
Company: Trailways (a noun in the dictionary)

Mnemonic scenario: The APE is meeting with *Jungle Jim* who will *"carry a gun"* on the TRAIL ALWAYS.

At 10:00 A.M. your appointment is with Jeffrey Close, a director at CIGNA, and you are to discuss company health care. Use WOODS, the code word for 10, and tie in the rest of the information this way:

Time:	10:00
Code word:	WOODS
Name:	Jeffrey (sounds like "jiffy")
	Close (a common dictionary word)
Company:	CIGNA (sounds a bit like "cigarette")
Topic:	Health care (Cigarettes are bad for health.)

Mnemonic scenario: The trees in the WOODS are very *close* together, and if someone dropped a CIGARETTE it would be hard on the *health* as the woods would go up in flames in a *jiffy*.

The morning moves along comfortably and you're ready for your 11:00 A.M. appointment with Merv Adelson at Lorimar-Telepictures, after which you plan to go to your health club and then have lunch with Marilyn Lewis at Hamburger Hamlet. Are you ready? I'll give you the lineup and you create the mnemonic connectors.

11:00	TIDE	Merv Adelson at Lorimar-Telepictures
12:00	TIN	Health Club
1:00	HAT	Lunch with Marilyn Lewis at Hamburger Hamlet

If you have appointments on the half hour, just add the word MOOSE to your code word and into your mnemonic scenario. MOOSE is the code word for 30. In the examples given, you could have Jungle Jim Kerrigan shooting MOOSE, a MOOSE who smokes cigarettes starting the fire in the WOODS, and Marilyn Lewis munching on MOOSE-burger at Hamburger Hamlet.

Although most appointments fall on the hour or half hour, if you do schedule something for the quarter hour, simply follow the same process and incorporate the code word HOTEL or RAIL for fifteen minutes past the hour and fifteen minutes before the hour respectively.

Take out your appointment book right now and practice by filing your own appointments for the day with the Master Mnumeric Code.

CONCLUSION

You can use the Master Code to mentally file and remember all important lists, whether they are appointments, names and territories of your sales force, the points you want to make in a speech or presentation. No matter how complex or simple, all lists can be triggered into your memory by the Master Code. Those lists that you need for permanent retention should be reviewed mentally from time to time to reinforce them. Temporary lists needn't be thought about when they are of no further use.

Review the code words themselves regularly to keep them functional. They should be as commonplace and useful as the index tabs in the office file drawer—but a lot more fun to use!

13

Remembering the News While It's Still News

The more you know, the more you're worth!

SCENARIO

You drive to the train station in the morning listening to the news report on the car radio. At the station you pick up today's *Wall Street Journal* and glance over the headlines. As the train pulls in you climb aboard, find a seat, loosen your coat, sit down, drop your briefcase between your legs, reach into a vest pocket, and pull out your felt-tip pen. Now you settle back for a half hour of what you call "serious reading." You learned how to do it in college when you didn't dare read a book without a yellow liner to highlight the important information. And you still do it. Your secretary teases you about being compulsive, but you claim you know better. "Got to stay on top of things," is the way you put it. "Doesn't staying on top of things sometimes get you down?" she asks. Nope. "What would you do if you forgot your felt-tip pen some morning?" You hadn't really thought about it. "Guess I'd just have to read without it . . . but somehow it just wouldn't be the same."

THE PROBLEM

We all have our little compulsive routines that to us seem like sacred rituals and to others seem like ruts. One of these, in whatever form it takes, is staying abreast of the latest developments in our professions and careers. The amount of written material that we know we should read increases at an alarming rate. The stack of books, magazines, and articles climbs higher toward the ceiling. Occasionally it slides off the corner of the desk. It's been suggested that we might actually be better off not reading everything we think we should read. Of course, we would have to fake it. After all, there comes a point in life when we can't admit publicly that we haven't read everything that everyone else has read ages ago.

You'll never be completely on top of all that you should read in the modern business world, but there is a way to make those mountains of reading easier to scale. By "reading mnemonically" you can toss the felt-tip pen away and relax while you peruse the morning paper. You can even listen to the radio and remember the lead stories without jotting them down. You'll be able to read office memos and business communications of all kinds and not need to take notes.

THE SOLUTION

You can take the stress out of reading and listening to the news each day by simply filing the key information in your Master Mnumeric File under the code words you've learned in the previous chapters. The idea is to comprehend each story thoroughly and tack the main thought or pertinent facts to a code word that will recall the news item for you when you need it. Remember that the mind works like a vast network of interconnected thoughts, ideas, and images. One thought ticks off another and so forth.

Often before I go on a radio program I mentally file the up-to-the-minute news stories that usually precede the talk shows. I enjoy surprising the radio hosts when I volunteer to give back the news stories that just aired. I offer to replay the news in the order it was presented or in any sequence they ask for. If they ask for the sixth story I can get right to it without starting at number one and counting up to six. On the other hand, if they tell me the main point of a given story, I can tell them in which numerical position it was broadcast. Even the news announcers are stunned when they hear me because they themselves usually can't remember every story or the order in which they read them. They ask me for the secret, but I tell them there is no secret. The difference is that I was mentally filing the stories and they were not!

Recently a broker from a firm I deal with heard me on ABC's New York-based "Owen Span Radio Show" and asked me how he could learn to pick up and retrieve the news so swiftly. I told him to send me a copy of that day's *Wall Street Journal,* with the news stories he found most important circled, and I'd use them as examples in this book. Here are the fifteen stories he selected. Read through them quickly, giving each one about the same amount of attention and time to sink in.

1. Eastern Airlines stock could take off, a few analysts say.
2. Mutual funds sales soared to $46.2 billion in the first half.
3. The Rockefellers plan to mortgage Rockefeller Center for $1.1 billion. Firm gets option to buy 60 percent and will offer securities to public.
4. Ashton-Tate plans to acquire Multimate International (which publishes a popular word-processing program) for $19 million.
5. Stock prices declined sharply as investors worried about interest rates and economy. Dow-Jones Industrial Average tumbled 13.20.
6. Medical insurance for travelers grows more popular.
7. BankAmerica is considering selling its nationwide consumer-finance unit, Finance-America Corp.
8. Japan-U.S. trade friction stirs fears of long and bitter battle.
9. Rhone-Paulenc, the French drug firm, hopes to begin clinical trials in U.S. of experimental AIDS drugs HPA-23.
10. Banks say problem loans to computer firms are growing.
11. Oil import taxes wouldn't be painless to the U.S. economy.
12. Castro presses his campaign to cancel Latin America's debts.

13. New M.B.A. graduates are lured to investment banking by high pay.
14. GM will locate complex for Saturn small-car project near Spring Hill, Tennessee.
15. Evening News Association is target of a hostile $453 million tender offer by entertainment executives Norman Lear and Jerrold Perenchio.

Now that you've glanced through all fifteen stories, let's go back and consciously index them for permanent filing. Already the information in each story has found a place in your subconscious memory—often a hiding place where it won't let you find it! This time we'll send each story to a particular place so you'll know where it is and how to retrieve it.

Any of the mnemonic strategies we've learned so far can be employed. You may have noticed as you read through the list the first time that certain visual or aural connections popped up automatically for some of the news stories. Why some and not others? Again, it all goes back to making information interesting and finding related images that give information more color and impact. Some of the stories were more dramatic or visual than others. You may have had a natural interest in some rather than others. The task for achieving *total* recall, however, is to create conscious interest in all of them, discover a mnemonic image or idea that will trigger each story for you, and file it in a particular place in your mental filing system where you can find it.

The more you use these memory techniques, the more they become play rather than work. You'll find yourself naturally noticing mnemonic connections and seeing relationships between what you want to remember and some-

thing you already know. Building bridges between the new
and the known will become second nature to you. Furthermore, you'll discover which of these techniques work best
for you. It isn't necessary to utilize all of them.

Here are the connective thoughts that I would make,
each incorporating the relevant information from the news
story and the code word that corresponds to the position
where I am filing it:

No. Code word	Story	Connective thought
1. HAT	Eastern takeoff	To remember the Eastern story I merely think about putting my best HAT on, boarding a plane and *taking off* for the *East*.
2. HONEY	Mutual funds sales soar	My HONEY and I have *Mutual fun* RuSHiN out to spend *billions*. (RuSHiN translates mnemonically to $462.)
3. HOME	Rockefeller Center	Too Too bad—*Rockefeller* has to mortgage HOME to buy SHoeS for the kids and offer them *security* in 2000. (The Too Too bad gives me the $1.1 billion and the SHoeS reminds me that the new company's interest will be 60 percent. The rest tells me there'll be security offerings.)

No. Code word	Story	Connective thought
4. HERO	Ashton-Tate Multimate Int'l.	My HERO *Ash*(ley) from Gone with the Wind is now a (po)-*ton-tate* and is having a *tête-à-tête* over a glass of TaB and it's the mm*m-ultimate*. (The tête-à-tête reminds me that Multimate is in word processing. The TaB is for the $19 million.)
5. HILL	Stock prices decline	I think of *stock prices* as little DeMoNS *tumbling down* the HILL. (DeMoNS tells me the Dow tumbled 13.20.)
6. SHOE	Travelers medical insurance	*Traveling* on foot makes my *feet hurt* and my SHOE is worn out. I need *medical insurance.*
7. COW	BankAmerica might sell Fin. Am. Corp.	*B of A* the sacred COW may decide not to *Finance America* anymore.
8. HIVE	Japan-U.S. trade	*Friction* in the HIVE between the bees as to who makes the best honeycombs, *Japan* or *U.S.*
9. APE	Rhone-Paulenc AIDS Drugs	APE is *rumbling* (sounds like Rhone-Paulenc) over the fact he has *AIDS*. He looks to *France* for a cure.

No. Code word	Story	Connective thought
10. WOODS	Computer loans	*Computers* growing everywhere in WOODS and they don't go a- *"lone"* to the *bank*.
11. TIDE	Oil import taxes	The TIDE is importing *oil* to the shore and it's *taxing* my toes.
12. TIN	Castro debts	*Castro* wearing a TIN star is trying to get away *without paying* the bill.
13. TEAM	M.B.A. graduates	*M.B.A. grads* joining the *investment banking* TEAM because they play for *higher stakes*.
14. TIRE	GM complex for Saturn	On *Saturday* I'm driving on my *GM* TIRE, which can *Spring* me right up the *Hill* to *Tennessee*. (The word "Saturday" will tick off Saturn.)
15. HOTEL	Evening News Assoc. is target	I'm relaxing in my HOTEL reading the *Evening News* but 2 strangers appear who have the *potential* (Perenchio) to *leer* (Lear) at and RiLe Me. (RiLe Me reminds me of the hostile $453 million tender offer. The words "potential" and "leer" remind me of Perenchio and Lear.)

Once all fifteen items are filed away, you can retrieve them as you need them.

It's often hard for me to believe it myself when I see how quickly and accurately I can grasp new information in great quantities like this. The mind's ear is what learns new information for us, and its ability to hold onto it is phenomenal.

For practice, try assimilating the following information from an article on Rolodex that appeared in *USA Today*. This should be a topic dear to your heart since the article pointed out that business people tend to be emotionally attached to their Rolodex files. The statistics listed below appeared in a sidebar next to the article. Using the Master Mnumeric Code, store all the specifics that you want to recall for future reference.

ABOUT ROLODEX

(Rolodex Corp. has an estimated 90% of the $30-million-plus-a-year desktop-file business.)

The company:

    Inventor: Arnold Neustadter in 1950

    Parent company: Insilco Corp., Meriden, Conn.

    Estimated sales: $27 million

    Products: 32 rotary files

              26 horizontal files

              35 kinds of Rolodex cards

              10 models Punchodex paper punchers

                2 software programs

    Current best-seller:

            VIP24C horizontal covered file which holds 500 cards, costs $23.25.

    Biggest file:

            6035X three-wheel rotary file which holds 6,000 cards, costs $212.50.

The main points or buzzwords are already indicated by the list headings: inventor, parent company, estimated sales, etc. Connect each of these to a code word in your MC. Put names into categories that will bring them back to you, and transpose all figures into words using the MA (the Mnumeric Alphabet). Last, create a thought or thought picture for each main point, hooking together all the information you've organized, and attach it to a card in your mental Rolodex.

CONCLUSION

If you had been reading this Rolodex article on the train this morning and using a mnemonic system like this, you could have relaxed en route, knowing you would remember all the pertinent information without marking up the article with a yellow highlighter. Let the article make its mark on your memory and you can dispense with marking up the article!

14

Mnemonics and the Stock Market

*Let mnemonics help you quote prices
as fast as the ticker tape.*

SCENARIO

You are reading the *Wall Street Journal, Barron's,* or the financial section of any major newspaper. Your eye floats down columns and bounces across lines of figures and letters. Without being aware of it, you're soaking up and digesting mnemonics. In fact, you might say that mnemonics is the language of American capitalism. AT&T, ITT, and GTE are mnemonics whose meanings you've routinely learned and memorized. You didn't have to consciously create either an acronym or acrostic for these companies. The financial world did it for you, and it makes life a lot easier. Almost all stock listings are handled in the same manner, either by an initialing mnemonic where only the first letter of each main word is used or a mnemonic abbreviation using one or more letters in the company name, such as Occi P for Occidental Petroleum and McDn D for McDonald Douglas.

THE PROBLEM

In a word: condensing great amounts of statistical information.

THE SOLUTION

Mnemonics. Why? Well, imagine the floor of the New York Stock Exchange without mnemonics! If the minds of the men and women who dart back and forth in the New York Stock Exchange are anything like the floor, you'd wonder how anything got traded. Clearly, the floor can tolerate clutter. The human mind cannot. Information has to be locked in neatly and quickly. It has to be readily available. And, as in the case of the market page of the newspaper, every square inch of space is important. There wouldn't be enough space to list all the trading and selling if mnemonics were not used.

The same is true of the conscious mind. Even though it seems the human memory has infinite storage capacity, the amount of retrievable information can be likened to an area with a limited amount of space. The more neatly, compactly, and systematically you store information, the easier you can fit it all in—and pull it out. Reducing long words and names to abbreviated mnemonics is the best way.

But leave it to the Wall Street people to go one step further and create mnemonics for mnemonics! The terms *Ginny Mae* and *Freddie Mac* are like second-generation mnemonics. Originally the Government National Mortgage Association and the Federal Home Loan Mortgage Corporation were referred to by their own abbreviations, GNMA and FHLMC. When both agencies issued securities, a mnemonic nickname was coined for each. Ginnie Mae is the mnemonic that sprung from GNMA, and Freddie Mac came from FHLMC.

Recently I received through the mail a brochure explaining Ginnie Maes that was loaded with mnemonics. After stating that the certificates were issued by the GNMA, it went on to say that these "represent a portion of a pool of FHA or VA guaranteed mortgages." Clearly, if mnemonics is the language of American business, one had better learn how to speak it, and speak it well.

DECIPHERING THE STOCK MARKET

Understanding the stock market, of course, goes beyond the ability to remember stock symbols. As in any high-powered industry or business, it means staying on top of constantly changing information, committing some of it to memory, and being able to retrieve it accurately.

Let's say you wanted to remember the NYSE's new lows listed in today's financial section. They would be listed with abbreviated versions of their full names:

Beker Ind.	Cigna
CampSoup	Interlogic
Purolator	RdBat
Transco Eng	

At this point, you have several mnemonic techniques for storing this kind of information. You could use the simple mental file or the Master Code Words. But the first approach that comes to my mind is simply to relate these terms to substitute words that could be put into a sentence.

This isolated mnemonic sentence would be enough to transfer the information on the newspaper page to my mind's
ear, where the companies would be locked into my short-
term memory. Here's how I would do it:

Beker Ind. reminds me of BAKER
Cigna reminds me of CIGAR
CampSoup is, of course, CAMPBELL SOUP
Interlogic gives me INTERESTINGLY and LOGI-
CALLY
Purolator, because it sounds like a mixer, gives me PUR-
OLATOR
RdBat suggests RED BAT
Transco Eng. sounds like TRANSIENT ENGINEERS

Now with these more complete words taking the places of
the company abbreviations, I can construct a sentence that
will hold them together for me.

"The BAKER smoked a CIGAR while mixing CAMPBELL
SOUP, INTERESTINGLY and LOGICALLY in a PUR-
OLATOR with his RED BAT in order to feed the
TRANSIENT ENGINEERS."

You may wonder if it takes some kind of daffy mind to
find sentences like this. Believe me, it does not! Being able
to spot the "hidden scenario" in a list of companies becomes
increasingly easy the more you do it. In fact, many executives have told me it's actually addictive. Once they learn
how to do it, they can't stop. They're constantly looking
for hidden images and mnemonic scenarios to make remembering easier.

Here's a way to keep up with the ups and downs of the stocks you regularly watch in order to get a feel for the climate in the market. Let's say the stocks you watch are these:

IBM	Merck
Exxon	Apple Computer
General Motors	Chase Manhattan Bank
American Tel and Tel	Burlington Northern
Delta Airlines	Long-term Treasury Bonds

To remember which ones are up and which are down each month, put all the ups in one group and the downs in another. Then take the initials of all the companies in the up group and devise an acronym or acrostic. Do the same with the initials of the companies in the down group. Each month simply devise a new acronym or acrostic to reflect that period's fluctuations. For example, if Exxon, General Motors, Apple Computer, and Delta are down, you could use the acronym EGAD.

Exxon	E
General Motors	G
Apple Computer	A
Delta	D

And if IBM, AT&T, Merck, Chase Manhattan, Burlington Northern, and Long-term Treasury Bonds are up, you could write the following acrostic sentence:

"I am married, could be love."

I	IBM
Am	AT&T
Married	Merck

Could	Chase Manhattan
Be	Burlington Northern
Love	Long-term Treasury Bonds

Note: I used "Am" in the acrostic so as not to confuse AT&T with Apple since they both begin with the letter A.

GETTING A MNEMONIC HANDLE ON STOCK PRICES

If you need to remember only one or two stock prices, you can use the simple techniques explained in Chapter 5 of letting the figures themselves kick off a mnemonic connection in your mind, such as famous dates, or finding some arithmetical relationship among the digits. But if you need to remember a great many prices, I suggest using the Mnumeric Alphabet to transpose the price into a translatory word or phrase.

When it comes to remembering fractions, the easiest way to get them down is to transpose them into eighths, which is the common denominator of all stock-price fractions. Use

$\frac{2}{8}$ for $\frac{1}{4}$
$\frac{4}{8}$ for $\frac{1}{2}$
and
$\frac{6}{8}$ for $\frac{3}{4}$.

All the others remain the same: $\frac{1}{8}$, $\frac{3}{8}$, $\frac{5}{8}$, $\frac{7}{8}$
For practice, take the following list of stocks

AT&T	up	$21\frac{1}{8}$
Burroughs	up	$78\frac{3}{8}$
Eastern	up	$24\frac{5}{8}$

Motorola	down	32¼
Robbins	down	18½
Armada	down	13¾
Beatrice	unchanged at	29⅞

If you could ignore the fractions, an easy way to commit these figures to memory would be with the associative technique of finding some significant "known" event or fact for each price. Here is how they would relate to me:

AT&T	21 - age of consent
Burroughs	78 - speed of an old record
Eastern	24 - hours in a day
Motorola	32 - famous football jersey
Robbins	18 - Army induction age
Armada	13 - unlucky number
Beatrice	29 - panic of

Next, I would make a further connection between the name of the stock and the price by finding a connective thought or scenario for each one.

AT&T	21	I can get my own "telephone"(AT&T) at the "age" (21) of consent.
Burroughs	78	"Burros" are as outmoded as an old "78" record.
Eastern	24	"Eastern" time seems to have more than "24" hours in a day.

Motorola	32	My football hero has a "motor" in his "jersey" (#32).
Robbins	18	All the "robins" are old enough to join the "army" (18).
Armada	13	The "armada's" coming to get us. "Bad luck" (13).
Beatrice	29	Poor "Beatrice" is in a "panic" (29).

If I decided to remember these quotes by using the mnumeric method—and I definitely would if I had to remember the fractions—I would transpose the fractions into eighths and phonetically translate only the numerator to a letter sound. Since you know that the denominators in all your remembered material are in eighths, you don't need to transpose them.

Using the Mnumeric Alphabet, I would convert the prices this way:

			2 1 1
AT&T	21⅛	into	NoTe iT
			7 8 3
Burroughs	78⅜	into	GiVe Me
			2 4 5
Eastern	24⅝	into	New RoLl
			3 2 2
Motorola	32⅜	into	MoaNiN'
			1 8 4
Robbins	18⅘	into	DiVeR

			1 3 6
Armada	13⁶⁄₈	into	DaMaGe
			2 9 7
Beatrice	29⁷⁄₈	into	No BuCk

The next step is to find a connective thought or picture that will link the price with the name of the stock. Here are my suggestions:

Stock	*Price*	*Translation*	*Connective thought*
AT&T	21⅛	NoTe iT	I heard it on the "telephone." I'll "note it."
Burroughs	78⅜	GiVe Me	"Give me" some "burros" to ride.
Eastern	24⅝	New RoLl	"Eastern" is on a "new roll."
Motorola	32²⁄₈	MoaNiN'	My "Motorola" is "moanin'."
Robbins	18⁴⁄₈	DiVeR	One of the "robins" is a "diver."
Armada	13⁶⁄₈	DaMaGe	The "armada" will do "damage."
Beatrice	29⅞	No BuCk	"Beatrice" has made "no buck" this week.

Here are some stocks and prices to try on your own. See how you do. (Remember to change *all* the fractions to eighths.)

Stock	*Price*	*Translation*	*Connective thought*
Data General	40¼	________	____________
Digital Equipment	99¼	________	____________

Intel	27¼	_____	_____
Texas Instruments	102½	_____	_____
Kellogg	53	_____	_____
General Foods	75⅞	_____	_____
Ralston Purina	41	_____	_____
Pillsbury	48⅝	_____	_____

Since not all the prices you deal with are stock prices, it may be good practice using the Mnumeric Alphabet on standard sales prices. For convenience, we'll use the previous stock names and figures but convert them into products and sales prices. In this way you'll see how widely the MA can be adapted across the board to handle all numerical needs and lists, whether you're dealing with market quotes, sales figures, service costs, or production statistics.

1.	Telephone plug	$ 2.11
2.	Toy burros	$ 7.83
3.	A ticket east	$245.00
4.	A motor	$322.00
5.	Mechanical robin	$ 1.84
6.	Army boots	$136.00
7.	Beets	$ 2.97

Lock this list into your master file by creatively connecting each item to a code word.

No.	Code	Product	Price	Translation
1.	HAT	Telephone plug	$2.11	(NoTe iT)
	I put my HAT by the telephone plug. I'll note it!			
2.	HONEY	Toy burros	$7.83	(GiVe Me)
	Give me two toy burros for my HONEY.			

No.	Code	Product	Price	Translation
3.	HOME	Ticket East	$245.00	(New RoLl)

I'm on a new roll and I'm buying a ticket East
to go HOME.

| 4. | HERO | A motor | $322.00 | (MoaNiN') |

My HERO is moanin' over the cost of a new motor.

| 5. | HILL | Mech. robin | $1.84 | (DiVeR) |

The robin on the high HILL is a diver.

| 6. | SHOE | Army boots | $136.00 | (DaMaGe) |

Wearing army boots for SHOEs will surely damage
my feet.

| 7. | COW | Beets | $2.97 | (No BuCk) |

The COW eating beets will give milk that earns
no buck.

If you're concerned about remembering where the decimal points go, create two separate words, one for the digits to the right of the decimal point and one for the digits to the left. For example, $2.11 would break down into two words: one to represent the digit 2 and the other to represent the number 11. We might use "No DebT" where "no" stands for 2 and "debt" stands for 11 (the *b* in the word *debt* is silent and therefore not valued).

For practice, think up other mnumeric translations for product prices 1, 2, 5, and 7 with separate words to show the split at the decimal point.

Here is one last exercise for perfecting the Master Mnumeric Code as a stronghold for prices and figures. According to an article on executive salaries in the magazine *Inc.*, manufacturing offers the highest pay for executives of the 516 privately owned companies surveyed with annual sales of $4.5 million. Here they are ranked from highest to lowest, waiting to be filed with your own personal mnemonic associations. Remember first to transpose the salaries into translatory words using the Mnumeric Alphabet, then relate these terms and the industry name to the code word with some connective thought or scenario.

Level	Code Word	Industry	CEO's salary
1	HAT	Durable mfg.	$ 114,652
2	HONEY	Nondurable mfg.	102,966
3	HOME	Service/Business	82,505
4	HERO	Construction	73,972
5	HILL	Service/Professional	72,960
6	SHOE	Finance/Insurance	71,631
7	COW	Wholesale/Retail	65,692

CONCLUSION

With the memory strategies that you now have under your belt, you should be able to tighten your hold on stock and other prices and statistics that change regularly. You need to be fast and accurate, but once you master these mnemonic techniques your memory will be primed for the task.

15

Making the Most of Seminars, Conferences, and Meetings

Time is money, but in most seminars time is just notes.

SCENARIO

You're sitting in another so-called "sensational" seminar and suffering the same self-doubts that you've come to call "seminar-alysis"—a numbing of the mind that brings into question your competence and talent, your interests, everything you used to rely upon for professional self-assurance. The company continues to spend bundles of money sending you to these gatherings and for what? You can't keep your mind on the speakers. Every one seems pompous or boring or both. Some of them seem young—too young. Maybe that's the problem. You know what they say about one's memory after a certain age. (You're certain you've passed that age.) You consider taking more detailed notes just so you won't go back to the office with nothing to report. But even your note-taking skills seem rusty. You start to scribble and realize that you missed what just came while you were writing what just went. You start to lean over a bit toward the person on your left whose pen has been whirling nonstop all over her yellow legal pad for the last hour. Maybe you can steal a few notes from her if you squint hard enough. But that seems like cheating. Then you feel like a kid in school who'd like to chuck it all and drop out.

THE PROBLEM

It *is* a question of dropping out. Not from school, of course. In fact, I've met many successful executives who really were high-school dropouts and then motivated themselves up the corporate ladder to the top of the business world. Now some of them give seminars!

The type of dropping out that creates a problem for attending seminars and conferences is not physical but mental. We become mental dropouts because of boredom or stress, both of which can occur when learning is not happening. In one sense, it is similar to the high-school dropout who thinks that teaching and learning are the same thing. They're not. Teaching can happen irrespective of learning. Just being exposed to teaching—or lecturing or speechifying—will not guarantee learning. The reason is that learning is an active verb. The learner must *do* something actively, creatively, consciously. And if we don't know what we must do, then we have to *learn how to learn.*

Taking notes is not the solution, even though it is a conscious and sometimes creative activity. While taking notes, the mind is diverted from learning by the act of note taking. The concentration on the physical act of writing gets in the way of genuine learning. When your hand starts to get cramped from pinching the pen too tightly, let that be a mnemonic signal that your mind is most likely also pinched and cramped!

Learning how to learn means understanding how the mind and memory work. Many companies and corporations first give their executives memory training before sending them to expensive seminars and conferences so they will get the most out of the material they will encounter. They need to learn creative ways to assimilate masses of information, glean the important points, and—most importantly—connect those points to relevant aspects of what they already know so they can apply them later back at the home company. As I've said before, we aren't born with memory skills to do this kind of thing. It's something that has to be learned.

True, we were born with eyes and ears, but they don't do the learning. In the business of learning, the eye, ear, and the *mind* must be partners. Mere reading or listening will not connect the information to the memory. You know how easy it is to read an entire page and discover when you get to the bottom that while your eye was on the page your mind was on the eighteenth hole, and you need to go back and read it again. The same phenomenon occurs while listening, especially to speeches and presentations that register high on the boredom scale. It has been estimated that 87 percent of what you hear is not retained twenty-four hours later. The mind's ear and the mind's eye must be made aware of what the physical senses are picking up. The message must be sent to the mind and welded in place with a connective thought.

The main problem is that our school systems don't really teach these skills. Some people pick them up on their own.

Others go through life thinking that learning will just "happen." Some of us live and die convinced that we were born with "poor" memories. But none of these fates is inevitable. Everyone can learn to use his or her memory to best advantage and reap the joys of seminars.

THE SOLUTION

The next time you attend a seminar or conference, you'll get a lot more enjoyment out of it if you arouse your mind's ear and eye. In fact, attending seminars can be fun if you make learning a process of discovery, if you make it an active and creative enterprise, one that goes beyond mere note taking.

If you feel better "listening with a pen and notepad," keep your notes short and to the point. Use only the speaker's key words. Be creative with mnemonic connections that they suggest to you so you can lock the information into your mind as well as onto the notepad.

If you are given written information to work from, break it down and organize it logically and mnemonically—that is, turn it into manageable chunks with connective cues that make sense to you. You seldom need to keep information in the same form or wording in which it is presented. Use your mnemonic skills to build connections from what is new to what is old *HAT*. Then file it in your simple file or into the Master Mnumeric File depending on its complexity.

The important principle behind attending seminars creatively is to take an *active* interest and role in assimilating the information. Don't just let it go in one ear and out the other. Don't turn it into meaningless scribbles in a note-book. You can raise your interest level in any material, no matter how dull, if you approach it mnemonically and actively index it into your memory. Then, as long as you keep your head on your shoulders, you may return to your office empty-handed (of notes) but not empty-headed (of ideas).

A SALES SEMINAR ON SUCCESSFUL CLOSING

For practice, assume you have just audited a sales seminar and want to lock in the thirteen steps toward a good closing. As the seminar draws to a close, you feel like the thirteen steps are closing in on you, and you need a surefire way to commit them to memory. Here they are:

1. Expect to close going into the session (that is, the law of assumed consent).
2. Obtain all available information about the prospective buyer from buying patterns to authority over decision making.
3. Preselect a presentation you can handle in keeping with the emotional makeup and needs of the buyer.
4. Provoke relevant curiosity and supply irresistible information.
5. Know your story and tell it with enthusiasm, confidence, and authority.
6. Use humor, creative language, and satisfied-customer anecdotes.
7. Don't engage in monologue; throw the buyer a lead and then listen and learn about him.
8. Avoid arguing.

9. Point out only exclusive features or services.
10. Supply the prospect with a reason for buying.
11. Maximize benefits; minimize cost.
12. Use testimonials.
13. Get the buyer to take part and sell himself.

Now, if this information were handed to you in written form or presented orally, your approach would be the same. Break each point down into the key ideas represented by buzzwords. Then connect the buzzwords to appropriate code words in your master file. Make the connection come alive in your mind with vivid images or scenarios. Here is how I would do it:

No. Code word	Buzz	Connective thought
1. HAT	Expect to close.	Take your HAT off to yourself, you CLOSED the deal.
2. HONEY	Know your prospect.	I want to KNOW everything about my HONEY (including her penchant for buying $).
3. HOME	Preselect your presentation.	You're at HOME practicing your PRESENTATION in front of a mirror.
4. HERO	Arouse curiosity and give irresistible information.	Ask your HERO how he got his medals and listen to his IRRESISTIBLE war stories.

No. Code word	Buzz	Connective thought
5. HILL	Know your story.	You're on the HILL telling and selling your STORY to the world.
6. SHOE	Use humor and creative language.	The SHOEshine man is making you LAUGH.
7. COW	Let him talk.	The COW is TALKING to you.
8. HIVE	Don't argue.	Get NASTY and the bees from the HIVE sting.
9. APE	Exclusive points.	Think of the EXCLUSIVE size of the APE.
10. WOODS	Supply reason for buying.	With the WOODS, you PLAY BETTER golf.
11. TIDE	Maximize benefits, minimize costs.	The high TIDE is at its MAXIMUM but there's MINIMAL DANGER.
12. TIN	Testimonials.	A TESTIMONIAL from the TIN man.
13. TEAM	Make him take part.	Get HIM on your TEAM.

If the same material were presented and the thirteen points did not have to be kept in a particular sequence, you could create an acrostic sentence such as the following for remembering the main points:

"I expect to close presently and have every reason to believe I shall."

The first letter of each word stands for a buzzword:

I	I	- INFORMATION	(get it all)
E	expect	- EXPECTATION	(ask for order)
T	to	- TESTIMONIALS	(have prepared)
C	close	- CURIOSITY	(arouse it)
P	presently	- PRESENTATION	(preselect)
A	and	- ARGUE	(don't)
H	have	- HUMOR	(use it)
E	every	- EXCLUSIVITY	(point it out)
R	reason	- REASON	(supply reason to buy)
T	to	- TALKING	(don't do it all)
B	believe	- BENEFITS	(maximize)
I	I	- INVOLVEMENT	(get him to take part)
S	shall	- STORY	(know it and show it)

A CONFERENCE ON MARKETING CONSULTING SERVICES

Let's take another example. Suppose you are at a business conference on how to market consulting services. The presenter begins to list and explain the potential needs a client might have for engaging a professional consultant. You're tired of taking notes and want to commit these twelve points to memory. Here's how you could do it. Just for practice, we'll assume you've locked the thirteen points for a successful closing into slots 1 through 13, so for these next points we will use the code words 14 through 25. This will strengthen and lengthen your immediate file. Here they are for review:

14 TiRe	18 DoVe	22 NuN
15 hoTeL	19 TuB	23 gNoMe
16 DiSH	20 NoSe	24 New yeaR
17 DoG	21 waND	25 NaiL

Now take the list of potential needs from the presentation and as you read each one decide which code word you can most easily and quickly associate it with. Since there is no sequential necessity here, you can decide which code word connects best with which idea. Remember, you'll acquire speed at doing this the more you practice it. Eventually, it will become second nature.

The connective thought between the remembered idea and the code word may be far-out, but don't make it so far-out that you have trouble reeling it back in.

Potential Needs of Client

Profitability
Employee motivation
Productivity
Decision-making capability
Marketing strategy
Public relations
Company morale
Management structure
Internal operations
Time management
Cash flow
Credibility in community

Here is a worksheet with the numbers and code words from the master file. I've filled in four of them to get you started.

No. Code word	Potential Need	Connective thought
1 4 14 TIRE	_____	_____
1 5 15 HOTEL	Employee motivation	Employees are MOTIVATED to party in the HOTEL.
1 6 16 DISH	_____	_____
1 7 17 DOG	_____	_____
1 8 18 DOVE	_____	_____
1 9 19 TUB	Cash flow	The CASH FLOWs out of the TUB along with the water.
2 0 20 NOSE	_____	_____
2 1 21 WAND	Client's credibility	I wave my magic WAND and a CLIENT appears. It's inCREDIBLE.

No. Code word	Potential Need	Connective thought
2 2 22 NUN	_____	_____
2 3 23 GNOME	_____	_____
2 4 24 NEW YEAR	Time management	It's that TIME again. Happy NEW YEAR!
2 5 25 NAIL	_____	_____

CONCLUSION

Now you're ready to attend your next seminar, armed with mnemonic strategies to make you an active and interested participant. Remember, *active interest* is the best way to stay on top of the material and retain it long after the seminar ends. All it takes is to go in with a range of code words already prepared; be alert to what is being presented; pick out the buzzwords or key thoughts; and connect them to the code words with a vivid, memorable connective scenario or statement.

16

Wrap-Up

The Bottom Line

People ask me if I ever forget anything. Sure, I do. I even forget where I laid my keys! Like everyone, I have a great memory when I use it and a lousy memory when I don't. A memory is like a suit of clothes. If you buy a new suit and let it hang in a closet, for all practical purposes you don't have a new suit of clothes. You won't be at ease in a fine restaurant if your fine clothes are at home. It's what you wear that counts, and even though clothes don't "make" us, as the old saying goes, they do give us the ability to fit into business and social situations. They make things possible.

The same is true of memory. Hanging in a closet, collecting dust, your memory is of little use. You find that it's impossible to remember even the simplest things. Memory skills have to be used if they are to work for you. They must be kept honed and polished, kept up to date, made relevant to your mental needs and challenges. Knowing that your memory strategies exist is not enough. Knowing that you once could remember long complicated lists won't do either. Memory skills follow the same rules as any other: use them or lose them.

You now know the method and have the means to motivate your memory. There is no mental challenge that cannot be overcome more easily through the application of the mnemonic principles you've practiced in these chapters. And Practice Makes Perfect. Creativity must be aroused and called to action. Conscious mnemonic connections are necessary to stimulate your memory, or you will be left to rely on learning by rote, which is tantamount to slow mental starvation. Remember that a "roting" memory is only one letter away from a rotting memory!

As a practical plan of action, organize and learn new information when you're fresh and alert, especially if your material is difficult or you have a great amount of data. Save the tired times for review. Everyone has personal high and low periods during the day. Be aware of your own and accommodate them. Don't force a lot of new information into your memory after lunch when you're sluggish or late in the day or even early in the morning if those are not peak times for you.

Use time well. Taking a little time up front to mentally store information will give you time later to review it while showering, jogging, driving, or falling off to sleep—wherever you are. You won't need to rely on books, papers, or written notes. You can save hours of needless rereading and feel secure at all times that you really know what you *do* know, as well as *what you don't know*.

Because mnemonics is a system, the principles of systems

analysis can be applied to it. It responds to the same kind
of strategy you would use in a corporate setting:

- Analyze and comprehend information before trying to
  remember it.
- Adapt and apply the mnemonic techniques according
  to each situation.
- Attend to accuracy first and speed second.
- Make the most of innovative ideas.
- Do all you can with what you've got.
- Assess and control each situation.
- Organize your program, and program your organiza-
  tion for maximum results.
- Set a goal for becoming an expert at mnemonic recall.
- Communicate your expertise to others.
- Think strategically and act keenly in the direction of
  achievement.
- Enhance your existing mnemonic system with creative
  adjustments when necessary.
- Apply specific knowledge about mnemonics to your
  preplanned objectives.

If you read all the chapters carefully, you may have
noticed that the overall strategy in each was basically
the same. It didn't matter whether the data to be remembered included names, lists, speeches, isolated facts,
foreign vocabulary, statistics, or phone numbers. Even
overcoming absentmindedness followed the same pattern.
The memory is always the memory no matter how difficult
or diverse the challenge. It will always work well if you
follow the principles on which it works. And they are
simple:

1. Turn your mental power on. Be alert and aware of what you want to remember.
2. Eliminate negative thinking. No more age jokes or I-have-a-bad-memory-for-this-or-that attitude.
3. Make mnemonic connections from the new to the known. Hear the connective thought in your mind's ear and see it with the mind's eye.
4. Organize and comprehend what you want to remember by using substitute words, acronyms, acrostics, mnumerics, or the indexed file in your mind.
5. Rethink and recognize the connection to set it firmly in your memory. This ensures positive recall.
6. Be positive about your ability to learn and remember.

To sum it up one last time—in a word—a *mnemonic* word, at that!—

M	Mental power on
E	Eliminate negativity
M	Mnemonics
O	Organization
R	Rethink and recall
Y	YES, you've got a great MEMORY!